# Economics

## for CSEC®

Peter Clavery • Rob Dransfield
Margaret Scott-Thompson

A Caribbean Examinations Council® *Study Guide*

# OXFORD
UNIVERSITY PRESS

Great Clarendon Street, Oxford, OX2 6DP, United Kingdom

Oxford University Press is a department of the University of Oxford. It furthers the University's objective of excellence in research, scholarship, and education by publishing worldwide. Oxford is a registered trade mark of Oxford University Press in the UK and in certain other countries

British Library Cataloguing in Publication Data
Data available

978-1-4085-1643-0

11

Printed and bound by CPI Group (UK) Ltd, Croydon, CR0 4YY

## Acknowledgements

**Cover:** Mark Lyndersay, Lyndersay Digital, Trinidad
www.Lyndersaydigital.com
**Illustrations:** Fakenham Prepress Solutions, Bridget Dowty (c/o Graham Cameron Illustration)
**Page make-up:** Fakenham Prepress Solutions, Norfolk

The author and the publisher would like to thank the following for permission to reproduce material:

**p2:** Art Directors & TRIP/Alamy; **p4:** Rolf Richardson/Alamy; **p6 & p8:** Shawn Banton/Nelson Thornes; **p10:** James Orr/Nelson Thornes; **p14:** Colin Babb/Nelson Thornes; **p16:** Colin Babb/ Nelson Thornes; **p18:** Wigton Windfarm Ltd; **p20:** Shawn Banton/Nelson Thornes; **p22:** Sandy Marshall/Nelson Thornes; **p24:** Sam Diephuis/Getty Images; **p26:** Rex Features; **p30:** Laurence Griffiths/Getty Images; **p32:** Rob Thompson/Nelson Thornes; **p34:** Howard Davies/Alamy; **p36:** Dave G. Houser/Alamy; **p38:** Blend Images/Alamy; **p40:** Art Directors & TRIP/Alamy; **p42:** James Orr/Nelson Thornes; **p44:** Don Despain/Alamy; **p48:** Shawn Banton/Nelson Thornes; **p58:** Ian Dagnall/Alamy; **p60:** Rob Thompson/Nelson Thornes; **p62:** Getty Images; **p64:** Fotolia; **p66:** David Neil Madden/Getty Images; **p68t:** Filipe Wiens/Alamy; **p68b:** Bon Appetit/Alamy; **p70:** Colin Babb/Nelson Thornes; **p72:** Enigma/Alamy; **p74:** iStockphoto; **p76:** Tristar Photos/Alamy; **p78:** Neil Cooper/Alamy; **p80:** iStockphoto; **p84:** John Gioannetti; **p86:** Art Directors & TRIP/ Alamy; **p88:** Joe Fox/Alamy; **p92:** Suzanne Long/Alamy; **p94:** money & coins@ian sanders/Alamy; **p98:** Lenox Quallo/Nelson Thornes; **p100:** Shawn Banton/Nelson Thornes; **p102:** Lenox Quallo/ Nelson Thornes; **p108:** Shawn Banton/Nelson Thornes; **p112:** Oliver Thornton/Nelson Thornes; **p114:** Dave G. Houser/Corbis; **p115:** United Nations Development Programme (UNDP); **p116:** Colin Babb/Nelson Thornes; **p118:** Sandy Marshall/Nelson Thornes; **p120:** Colin Babb/Nelson Thornes; **p124:** Art Directors & TRIP/Alamy; **p128:** Rob Thompson/Nelson Thornes; **p130:** Mike van der Wolk/Nelson Thornes; **p134:** Lenox Quallo/Nelson Thornes; **p136:** money & coins@ian sanders/Alamy; **p138:** Arko Datta/Reuters; **p140:** Fotolia; **p144:** Hemis.fr/SuperStock; **p150:** Rob Thompson/Nelson Thornes; **p152:** MCP/Rex Features; **p155:** Paul Thompson Images/Alamy; **p158:** Rob Thompson/Nelson Thornes; **p160:** incamerastock/Alamy; **p164:** Piluhin/Alamy; **p166:** Rob Thompson/Nelson Thornes; **p168:** Oliver Thornton/Nelson Thornes; **p170:** Elisabeth Peters/Alamy; **p172:** Sandy Marshall/Nelson Thornes; **p174:** vario images GmbH & Co.KG/Alamy; **p176:** Mike van der Wolk/Nelson Thornes; **p178:** Eye Ubiquitous/Glowimages; **p180:** AXSES Web Communications.

Although we have made every effort to trace and contact all copyright holders before publication this has not been possible in all cases. If notified, the publisher will rectify any errors or omissions at the earliest opportunity.

Links to third party websites are provided by Oxford in good faith and for information only. Oxford disclaims any responsibility for the materials contained in any third party website referenced in this work.

# Contents

# Contents

This Study Guide has been developed exclusively with the Caribbean Examinations Council (CXC®) to be used as an additional resource by candidates, both in and out of school, following the Caribbean Secondary Education Certificate (CSEC®) programme.

It has been prepared by a team with expertise in the CSEC® syllabus, teaching and examination. The contents are designed to support learning by providing tools to help you achieve your best in Economics and the features included make it easier for you to master the key concepts and requirements of the syllabus. *Do remember to refer to your syllabus for full guidance on the course requirements and examination format!*

Included with this Study Guide is an interactive CD which includes electronic activities to assist you in developing good examination techniques:

- **On Your Marks** activities provide sample examination-style short-answer and essay-type questions, with example candidate answers and feedback from an examiner to show where answers could be improved. These activities will build your understanding, skill level and confidence in answering examination questions.
- **Test Yourself** activities are specifically designed to provide experience of multiple-choice examination questions, and helpful feedback will refer you to sections inside the Study Guide so that you can revise problem areas.

This unique combination of focused syllabus content and interactive examination practice will provide you with invaluable support to help you reach your full potential in CSEC® Economics.

# The creation of wealth

Fish are a scarce natural resource, and the Caribbean fishing industry creates wealth

Economics is a social science. Social sciences examine human society. Economics is the study of how people in this human society create wealth. A widely used definition of economics is that it is the study of how wealth is created from the allocation of scarce resources.

This definition introduces two important ideas:

• Resources are scarce: these may be natural resources such as oil or fish. There is a limited supply of oil and edible fish in the Caribbean Sea.

• Resources can be used to create wealth: fish provide a rich and varied diet, but in addition the fishing industry provides income for fishermen. The fishermen in turn pay taxes which enable the government to provide, for example, hospitals and schools.

Fish and oil are both natural resources. The Caribbean Sea is teeming with a variety of edible fish, for example red snapper, marlin, grouper, catfish. Oil is found beneath the sea bed and the oil industry brings wealth to some countries, particularly Trinidad. Thousands of workers are employed in the oil industry. Oil is the single biggest natural resource export from the Caribbean, with the United States its main market.

However, as we shall see in 1.3, oil and fish are not **free goods** (as opposed to **economic goods**). They need to be extracted, and time and resources have to be invested, for example to build the fishing boats and oil rigs required to do this. To create wealth from natural resources, investment is required. Investment involves giving up something in the short term in the hope of increasing wealth in the longer term. Investment may be of time or of money.

## Production and distribution of goods and services

Production consists of all the processes required to make goods and services. For example, fish can be caught on the line or in a net, but will often go through the process of being cleaned and filleted before being sold. In the oil industry, production begins with the exploration for oil fields. When oil is found, the process of constructing oil rigs begins, to enable the extraction of the oil.

The next stage is the distribution of the fish to the fish market and the oil to the oil terminal. At the market the fish is sold to shops, restaurants and private customers. From the terminal the oil can be refined to make petroleum and other products. Figure 1.1.1 illustrates the production of oil.

Each of the stages in Figure 1.1.1 involves production. Production involves making a good more valuable to the end consumer. Distribution involves getting the goods to where they are needed. In the oil industry, distribution involves making goods available to the motorist, for example. This includes transporting it by pipeline or oil tanker. Storing the oil and selling it at a service station are also part of the distribution process.

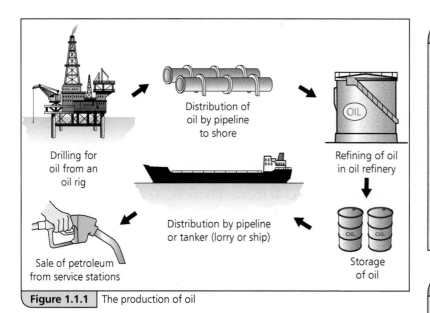

| | |
|---|---|
| Drilling for oil from an oil rig | Distribution of oil by pipeline to shore |
| | Refining of oil in oil refinery |
| Sale of petroleum from service stations | Distribution by pipeline or tanker (lorry or ship) |
| | Storage of oil |

**Figure 1.1.1** The production of oil

## Interactions involved in creating wealth

Creating wealth involves many people interacting in production activity. In our examples, these may include the fishermen, oil workers, transport workers and retailers. Interactions are also required between the buyers and sellers of the products. The welfare of these individuals depends on how well the economic system is working.

When more goods are produced, many consumers find that there are more goods available to buy. When production increases, people's incomes rise. As we shall see in 1.2, Caribbean economies will grow as the production and distribution systems become more efficient over time.

Table 1.1.1 shows definitions of the terms introduced in this topic.

**Table 1.1.1** Important economic definitions

| Wants Goods and services that individuals desire to own and use | Needs Items that people require to survive, including basic foodstuffs, shelter and basic clothing |
|---|---|
| Goods Tangible (touchable) items such as food and household goods | Services Intangible services provided for people, businesses and government, e.g. insurance and banking services |
| Wealth A stock of valuable items, e.g. a house, car, and money in the bank that has been built up over a period of time | Income A new flow of money that is earned in a given period of time (income that is saved can be used to build up wealth) |

# The economy

Candidates should be able to:

• explain what is meant by an economy

• list the main sectors in the economy.

Tourism plays an important part in generating income for the St Kitts and Nevis economy

Entrepreneurs play a key part in any economy. They are the people who bring the other resources together to produce goods and services, for example a hotel owner. Entrepreneurs are risk-takers because they cannot be sure that their business ventures will succeed.

## The economy as a system

The economy is a system that creates wealth. Economic systems exist at a number of levels: we can refer to the global economy, or to the Caribbean economy or, at a local level, to the economy of St Kitts and Nevis. The economy of St Kitts and Nevis creates jobs and incomes for people on these islands and trades with other Caribbean countries and the wider world.

An economic system:

• organises resources for the production of goods and services

• satisfies the wants and needs of people who are part of that system.

The economic system helps society to answer the 'three economic questions':

1 What goods and services should be produced (consumption)?

2 How are they to be produced and in what quantities (production)?

3 Who should receive the goods (distribution)?

| **CASE STUDY** | The economy of St Kitts and Nevis |
| --- | --- |

The economy of St Kitts and Nevis uses scarce resources to produce valuable commodities. People on these islands produce goods and services which are then distributed to consumers through retail and other outlets. The goods and services that are produced and distributed help to satisfy many of the territory's inhabitants.

Traditionally the main activity in the economy of St Kitts and Nevis revolved around the sugar cane industry. Sugar cane was cultivated and harvested. It was then refined into sugar. Much of this sugar was exported to other countries. However, as a result of falling world sugar prices, the industry became less important.

In recent years the government of St Kitts and Nevis has sought to diversify the economy. New industries that have been successful include offshore banking and tourism. Offshore banks are places where people (in this case often from the United States) can keep their money without paying the taxes they would need to pay at home. To encourage tourism, hotels and restaurants have been developed on the islands as well as watersports activity centres. The resources that are used in this industry include natural resources such as sandy beaches and the ocean, physical resources such as buildings or watersports equipment and human resources (the people who work in hotels and restaurants).

Hurricanes have had a devastating effect on the economy of St Kitts and Nevis at different times. Hurricanes affect the ability of the economic system to produce and distribute goods. They can destroy wealth in the form of roads, buildings and people's homes.

### Questions

**1** Give three examples of resources that will be used in the offshore banking industry in St Kitts and Nevis. (Hint: What resources does the case study mention were used in tourism?)

**2** St Kitts and Nevis is described as an economy. What do you understand by this term?

## The main sectors in the economy

There are three main sectors in any economy:

- firms
- households
- government.

In St Kitts and Nevis there are many small companies, for example in the clothing industry and in the assembly of electronic products. There are also farms and retail outlets. Firms employ labour and pay taxes to the government.

Households play an important part in the economy. They provide labour for firms and householders consume the products made by the firms.

The government also plays an important part in the economy. For example, until 2005 many people in St Kitts and Nevis worked for the government-run sugar corporation.

Today the government provides jobs in public administration, education, police and other services. Firms and households pay taxes to the government. The government provides important services such as education and health services (Figure 1.2.1).

The government will seek to ensure that the economy grows over time. When the economy of St Kitts and Nevis grows, it will be able to produce more goods and services and people will be able to enjoy more wealth. The government in turn will receive more taxes and be able to provide more services.

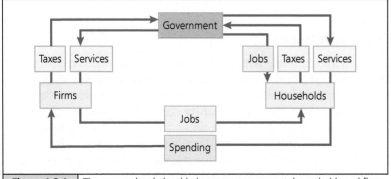

**Figure 1.2.1** The economic relationship between government, households and firms

# Scarcity and choice

Candidates should be able to:

- explain the concept of scarcity and choice within an economy
- define 'opportunity cost' and 'money cost'.

Scarce land can be used for farming, housing or as a cricket ground

**EXAM TIP**

A 'shortage' of a good is different from a 'scarcity'. A shortage occurs when the demand for a good exceeds supply: this can be solved. Scarcity, however, will always exist because wants will always exceed the availability of resources to satisfy them.

## The concepts of scarcity and choice

Economists talk of the 'basic economic problem': there are never enough resources for everyone to have everything that they want. Choices have to be made. There are several types of resource (Figure 1.3.1).

| Natural resources | Man-made resources | Human resources |
|---|---|---|
| soil, climate, water, minerals, forests and fisheries | machinery, buildings and equipment | people and their skills |

**Figure 1.3.1** Types of resources

If society had all the land, labour, raw materials and other resources it needed, we could produce all the goods we wanted without making sacrifices. In reality resources are scarce. When we use resources to produce an item, we are taking away those resources from the production of something else. This is a major problem for all societies.

Decision-making over the use of resources involves:

- making a choice (we can do one thing *or* the other)
- making a sacrifice (if we choose to do one thing with a resource, we cannot also do another).

A good example of scarcity and choice in the Caribbean is the use of land. In island economies there is relatively little land, so choices have to be made about how to use it. Choices include agriculture, housing, recreational facilities (for example cricket grounds) or industrial use.

## Opportunity cost

We often ask someone with a new purchase 'How much did it cost?' We are asking how much was paid for it – that is, the money cost. However, in economics we use a slightly different meaning of 'cost'. Economists believe that **opportunity cost** reveals the 'real cost' of making a choice. For example, when you choose to buy a new computer game, the sacrifice that you are making is the next best thing that you could have spent the money on. The real cost of any choice is therefore the alternative that is sacrificed.

# A production possibility curve

In an economy it is only possible to produce a given number of goods at a particular moment in time. The number that can be produced is the **production possibility curve** (or frontier). This shows combinations of goods that can be produced in an economy at a particular time, utilising all resources. For example, a territory could use its land to grow two main types of crop – bananas or sugar. If it used all the land to grow bananas it could grow 100 000 kilos per year. Alternatively it could use all of its land to produce sugar and produce 50 000 kilos per year. A third choice would be to use some of the land for growing bananas and some for growing sugar. For every extra kilo of bananas grown the economy would have to give up half a kilo of sugar. If each area of land was identical, the production possibility curve would be a straight line (Figure 1.3.2).

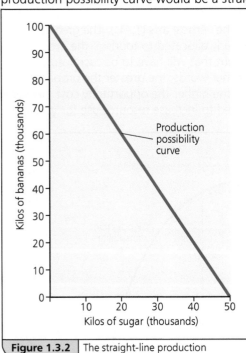

**Figure 1.3.2** The straight-line production possibility curve: substituting sugar for bananas where land is identical

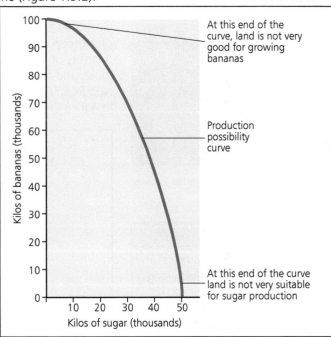

At this end of the curve, land is not very good for growing bananas

Production possibility curve

At this end of the curve land is not very suitable for sugar production

**Figure 1.3.3** The curved production possibility curve: substituting sugar for bananas where some land is more suitable for banana and some for sugar production

However, land is not identical. Some land is more suitable for growing bananas and some for sugar. If farmers want to produce more bananas they will first use the land that is best for growing bananas and least good for growing sugar. In this case the production possibility frontier is a curve rather than a straight line. The nearer we are to the end of the curve the steeper it is, because to grow more of one crop will involve a greater sacrifice of the other. The more bananas we grow, the larger the reduction on sugar output required to produce a few more bananas.

## KEY POINTS

- Goods and services are scarce relative to wants and needs for them.
- Opportunity cost is the next best alternative that is sacrificed when a choice is made.
- A production possibility curve illustrates combinations of two goods that can be produced with available resources.

## SUMMARY QUESTIONS

1 What is the opportunity cost to a farmer of using his or her land to grow bananas?

2 What is the opportunity cost to the government of building a school?

# Opportunity cost and efficiency

To convert agricultural land to hotels involves giving up agricultural output

## Illustrating opportunity cost

The concept of opportunity cost can be illustrated in the form of production possibility curves (see 1.3). In the production possibility curve shown in Figure 1.4.1 an island can use its land for one of two purposes – for tourism or for agricultural production. To convert agricultural land to hotels and leisure activities will involve giving up some agricultural output. The distance shown by the arrow ($A_1$–$A_2$) on the horizontal axis shows the value of agricultural production sacrificed to increase the value of tourism income by the value illustrated by the arrow on the vertical axis ($T_1$–$T_2$). The greater the proportion of resources already allocated to tourism, the greater the quantity of agricultural output that will have to be sacrificed to use more land for tourism. In other words, the greater the proportion of resources used for tourism, the higher the opportunity cost measured in agricultural output required to increase resource use for tourism.

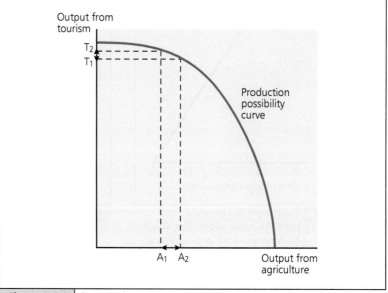

**Figure 1.4.1** | Opportunity cost

## Illustrating efficiency

The production possibility curve illustrates how much can be produced of two goods assuming that all resources are being fully employed. For example, on the production possibility curve shown in Figure 1.4.2, points A, B and C show combinations of agricultural and tourism output that could be produced assuming all resources are fully employed. However, points D, E, and F illustrate points where some resources are not being used. D, E and F thus represent inefficient situations where some resources are unemployed. Point G is not possible given existing resources.

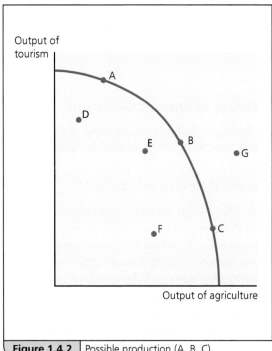

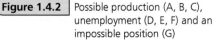

**Figure 1.4.2** Possible production (A, B, C), unemployment (D, E, F) and an impossible position (G)

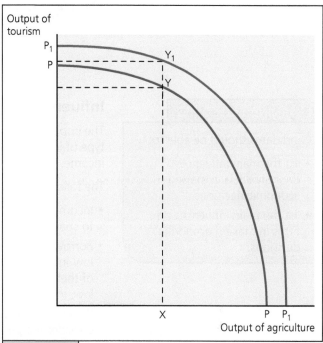

**Figure 1.4.3** Increased efficiency

## Illustrating growth

Over time economies become more efficient. This generally results from investing resources, for example by building new hotels or investing in new agricultural equipment. Increased efficiency is represented by a movement in the production possibility curve to the right. Assuming the original frontier is the curve PP, increased efficiency is represented by $P_1P_1$. To illustrate that $P_1P_1$ is more efficient, look at a point where 'x' of agricultural goods is produced. On PP only 'Y' of tourism output can be produced. However, on $P_1P_1$ '$Y_1$' of tourism output can be produced (Figure 1.4.3).

The production possibility curve could also move from $P_1P_1$ to PP. For example, the economy could become more inefficient as a result of a hurricane. Two main factors affect the production possibility curve: a change in the amount of resources and a change in the productivity of existing resources.

**EXAM TIP**

A production possibility curve shows combinations of two goods that can be produced with existing resources. It can shift to the right when those resources become more efficient or there are more resources. It will shift to the left if the resources become less efficient or there are fewer resources.

### KEY POINTS

• Opportunity cost can be illustrated on a production possibility curve by showing the sacrifice resulting from producing more of one good.
• A shift outwards in the production possibility curve results from increasing efficiency in production.

### SUMMARY QUESTIONS

1 What do points on a production possibility curve represent?

2 What is represented by points:

   a to the left of the curve?
   b to the right of the curve?

# Making economic decisions

Candidates should be able to:

- list the main influences on individuals in making economic decisions
- list the main influences on firms in making economic decisions.

## Influences on individual economic decisions

The important economic decisions that individuals make are what type of job to do, whether to spend or save and how to spend their income.

The following factors influence these economic decisions:

- Income: when income and/or wealth increases, individuals are able to spend more. They can also save more.
- Borrowing: high-income earners can afford to borrow more than low-income earners. They are also likely to save a higher proportion of their income than low-income earners. Where incomes are very low, individuals might have to borrow money to buy essentials.
- Wealth: in making individual economic decisions, people will consider the prices of various goods available to them. Richer people will be able to buy more goods and higher-priced goods. Poorer people will often have to buy fewer goods and at lower prices.
- Changes in the rate of income tax: when tax rates rise, individuals' disposable income falls, and they may cut back their spending as a result.
- Taste: tastes influence individual economic decisions. When tastes change in favour of goods and services, more is spent on these – fashionable clothes, for example.

### DID YOU KNOW?

Consumers, producers and governments have different motives for making economic decisions: consumers seek to purchase goods that give them value for money; producers aim to make a profit; and governments want to create stability in the economy with steady growth of incomes and spending.

The size of a person's income determines their consumption (and how much they save)

| CASE STUDY | Clive and Pearline |
| --- | --- |

Clive is a lawyer in his 40s working in the law courts in Kingston, Jamaica. Pearline has recently left school and started work as a junior office clerk. Clive has worked and saved for many years and is now a wealthy person. Pearline is just starting out and has had to take a small loan from the bank. She has many essential purchases to make, such as the bus fare to work and smart clothes for the office. Because Clive has a high income he is able to save money and spend on luxuries for himself and his family, such as a large car and expensive holidays. As a high earner he pays income tax at a higher percentage in the dollar than Pearline.

Clive's and Pearline's spending is in some ways influenced by their tastes. For example, Clive's taste in clothes is a little more old-fashioned than Pearline's.

### Questions

1 How do Clive's and Pearline's incomes affect their spending?

2 Who is able to save more and why?

3 How might Clive's or Pearline's tastes change? What would be the effect on their spending?

4 If Clive's rate of income tax increased, what might be the impact on his spending?

## Influences on producers in making economic decisions

Producers need to decide what goods to produce and in what quantities. The decisions they make are influenced in turn by the buying, spending and saving decisions made by individuals.

The key influences on producers' decisions are:

• the resources available to them
• the budget available to them
• technical know-how.

A business needs suitable resources. In the Caribbean, fishing is popular because there are natural resources (fish) available and the only equipment required is a fishing boat, a reel and line. Tourism is also possible where there are resources in the form of sandy beaches and a favourable climate.

However, to catch fish and to operate tourist facilities, producers need to have a budget (money) available. A fishing boat is an expensive purchase, and a hotel or restaurant is a large investment. To set up a taxi business, for example, an enterprising person must be in a position to borrow the funds to buy a car and keep it running.

Having the right technical know-how is also needed before setting up production. A fisherman needs to know how to operate an outboard motor for a fishing boat. To set up a small factory outlet requires technical expertise in production skills. So in deciding whether to set up as a producer it is important to answer certain questions:

• Do I have access to the right resources?
• Is my budget sufficient for what I want to do?
• Do I have, or can I acquire, the necessary technical know-how?

**KEY POINTS**

• The main influences on individual economic decision-making are the income available to a person and the prices of goods.
• The main influences on economic decisions made by producers are resources available, budget and technical know-how.

**SUMMARY QUESTIONS**

1 What are the main influences on you as an individual in making economic decisions?

2 What are the main influences on a business that processes food in making economic decisions?

## SECTION 1: Multiple-choice questions

1 Michelle has $20 and can buy a CD, a new shirt or a bracelet. She must choose between the CD or the bracelet. In the end she chooses the bracelet. The opportunity cost is:

   a  $20

   b  The next best alternative that was sacrificed in making the buying decision

   c  The price of the bracelet

   d  The new shirt that she could have bought with her $20

2 The production possibility curve illustrated here shows combinations of sweet potatoes and peppers that could be grown on a given area of land. Which combination of sweet potatoes and peppers provides the most efficient combination given existing resources?

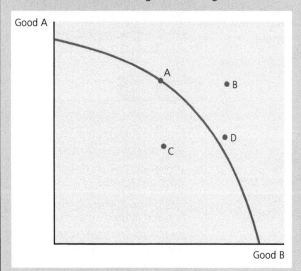

3 Which of the following is not a natural resource?

   a  Capital

   b  Land

   c  Oil

   d  Fish

4 Economics is the study of:

   a  How natural resources are created

   b  How societies make choices

   c  How goods and services are produced

   d  How people create wealth using scarce resources

5 A production possibility curve shows potential outputs of two goods, fishing and agriculture. The opportunity cost of producing one more unit of agricultural output in terms of fishing output will be:

   a  Constant along the length of the curve

   b  Greater the more agricultural goods are already produced

   c  Less the more agricultural goods are already produced

   d  Impossible to calculate because it will fluctuate so much

6 Garey owns a taxi that takes passengers from Grantley Adams Airport in Barbados to hotels on the island. When he carries passengers in his cab he is providing them with:

   a  A tangible benefit

   b  A good

   c  An intangible income

   d  A service

7 Which of the following is the best example of a free good?

   a  An inexpensive item such as salt

   b  A good that is not widely available

   c  Something that is not scarce relative to the demand for it

   d  A good that is given away in a two-for-the-price-of-one offer

8 Every month Margaret saves $100 from her income. As a result:

   a  She is not faced by any economic problems

   b  Her stock of wealth is increasing

   c  There is no opportunity cost involved in her saving

   d  She does not have to make choices

**9** The production possibility curve for Cuba has shifted steadily to the right during the last 20 years. An explanation for this might be:

a Cuba is subject to periodic hurricanes

b The Cuban economy is growing

c There are frequent shortages in Cuba

d Cuba does not produce many economic goods

**10** Scarcity results from:

a The supply of all goods being greater than the demand for them

b The existence of a large number of free goods

c Resources being insufficient to meet wants and needs

d The efficient use of free goods in the economy

## SECTION 2: Structured questions

**1 a** Define *opportunity cost*. (*2 marks*)

b Give one example of how a decision that a consumer makes will involve an opportunity cost. (*2 marks*)

c Give one example of how a decision that the government makes will involve an opportunity cost. (*2 marks*)

d A country can use its land to build shops and offices or as agricultural land. Draw a production possibility curve that illustrates the opportunity cost of building more shops and offices in terms of agricultural land. (*4 marks*)

e Explain the concepts of scarcity and choice in relation to the production possibility curve that you drew in part (d). (*5 marks*)

**2 a** Define the term *economics*. (*2 marks*)

b List the three sectors of the economy. (*3 marks*)

c Explain how one of these sectors helps to create wealth in the economy. (*3 marks*)

d Describe ways in which both distribution and production contribute to the creation of wealth in an economy. (*7 marks*)

**3 a** Define the terms *wants* and *needs*. (*2 marks*)

b How does the economy help to meet wants and needs? (*4 marks*)

c Draw a diagram (showing two production possibility curves) and explain it showing how increased productive efficiency can lead to more wants and needs being satisfied. (*5 marks*)

d Explain two ways in which an economy could become more efficient. (*4 marks*)

**4 a** Describe two ways in which an increase in an individual's income may affect the economic decisions that they make. (*4 marks*)

b Outline two motivations that affect the way that a government is involved in the economy. (*4 marks*)

c Describe two ways in which the government interacts with producers in the economy. (*6 marks*)

d Explain two ways in which producers help consumers to have their wants and needs met in the economy. (*6 marks*)

**5 a** Define a *production possibility curve*. (*2 marks*)

b Illustrate a production possibility curve for two agricultural products, and explain the shape of the curve. (*6 marks*)

c Illustrate and explain how the production possibility curve might alter as a result of a hurricane. (*6 marks*)

d Explain how a production possibility curve might shift outwards. (*6 marks*)

## 2.1     Production

Hairdressers provide an intangible service

### Goods and services

One of the major functions of the economy is to produce goods and services. A good typically means a physical item such as a bag of sugar, a pencil or a laptop computer. Some goods are referred to as 'consumer goods' because they are used by consumers, for example food items such as a bag of rice. Other goods are referred to as producer goods, for example a machine in a factory used by the producers of goods.

In contrast, services are intangible items that meet consumer and producer needs. 'Intangible' means that you cannot physically touch the service. Examples of services include banking, insurance and transportation services. In each of these examples the customer is paying the producer to provide a service for them – to look after their money, to cover their insurance risks or to transport something for them. Services are bought both by individuals and by businesses.

### Production and productivity

Production consists of the processes involved in providing goods and services. Each stage in production adds value to the good or service being produced. This process of producing a good can be illustrated in the production of fresh orange juice (Figure 2.1.1).

**Productivity** is a measure of the output that can be obtained from using productive resources. For example, if 10 employees can produce 100 units of output in an hour, their productivity is 10 units per employee hour. Productivity can be increased by the employees working harder or by working with improved resources. For example, if the 10 employees work with new, more advanced machinery they may be able to produce 200 units in an hour, as shown in Table 2.1.1.

**Table 2.1.1 Productivity at different output levels**

|  | Working with old machinery | Working with new machinery |
| --- | --- | --- |
| Number of employees | 10 | 10 |
| Hourly output | 100 | 200 |
| Productivity per employee (per hour) | 10 | 20 |

| Stage of production: | How value is added |
|---|---|
| **1** Growing the oranges  | Farmers look after the orange trees for several years before they give fruit. Each year they must be treated against pests. |
| **2** Transporting the oranges  | Fresh ripe oranges are transported closer to market. |
| **3** Preparing the oranges  | The juice is squeezed from the oranges and ice added. |
| **4** Serving the customer  | The juice is presented to the end consumer in a polite and friendly way. |

**Figure 2.1.1** | Adding value to a product: the customer benefits from value being added at each stage of production

Productivity can be measured either in real terms, that is units of output produced per unit of input, or in money terms, that is the money value of output per unit of input. For example, if we wanted to measure the productivity of a machine we could record this in the following ways:

- the physical output method, for example 200 units per machine hour
- the revenue output method, for example $1000 per machine hour.

(In our example we are assuming that each physical unit is sold for $5.)

### LEARNING OUTCOMES

Candidates should be able to:

- define the term *factors of production*
- identify the economic resources referred to as factors of production
- state the rewards of factors of production.

'Labour' is employees working to serve customers

### DID YOU KNOW?

The reward to labour is wages; the reward to enterprise is profit; the reward to capital is interest; and the reward to land is rent.

Factors of production are the four main types of economic resources that are combined to produce goods and services. The factors are land, labour, capital and enterprise.

## The four main factors

Imagine that you are visiting a modern travel agency. What do you see? The most obvious sight will be the premises themselves, in which there will be a number of employees sitting behind desks with easy access to computer terminals, and brochures giving details about holidays and tours.

The factors of production are what make the business work: land, labour, capital and enterprise.

- In the travel agency the land includes the site on which the offices are built.
- The labour is the employees working to serve customers.
- The capital is the buildings and machinery, in this case the office itself and the various computer terminals.
- Enterprise is the factor that takes the risk in bringing the factors together to produce the travel service in order to make profits.

## Definitions

Over the years the four factors of production have come to mean more than the examples used above:

- Land now refers to all natural resources, for example farmland, water, oil.
- Labour refers to all the physical and intellectual contributions of an employee. So it is more than just the physical effort of fishing or making car parts – it also includes the mental effort of an accountant or the services provided by a bank clerk.
- Capital includes all the items that go into producing other things. For example, a machine manufactures products, tools contribute to this process, and so on. Machines, tools and buildings are all examples of physical capital.
- Enterprise is the factor that brings the other factors together to produce goods in order to make profits.

Factors of production earn rewards for their use in production. The more valuable the service that a factor provides, the higher the reward is likely to be.

Indar Weir is a well-known entrepreneur from Barbados. He has worked in the Caribbean tourism industry for almost 40 years. In 1997 he set up the Indar Weir Travel Centre in Bridgetown to package holidays for the cricket World Cup. His company operates a Caribbean tourism and business advisory service. The business sells a range of services including holidays, cruises, car rentals and weddings.

To run his enterprise Indar Weir rewards certain features:

- Labour with wages: attractive salaries and wages are paid to employees in the Travel Centre.
- Land with rent: Indar Weir has to pay rent on some of the sites on which his agencies are located.
- Capital with interest: like most other businesses, Indar Weir borrows money from banks to fund purchases of equipment or facilities used by the business. Interest must be paid at regular intervals on the loans.
- Enterprise with profits: profits are a reward for enterprise. The profits of Indar Weir are shared out among shareholders in the business (or reinvested in the business).

### Questions

1 Which factor is responsible for bringing together the other factors of production? What is the reward for that factor?

2 Why is labour important to a travel business?

### EXAM TIP

You should be able to list the four factors of production and identify the rewards to each of these factors. Make sure that you understand the role of the entrepreneur in bringing these factors together and in taking risks.

The Indar Weir case study provides a good example of how the factors of production can be combined to create production. Indar Weir is a successful entrepreneur because he was able to spot new opportunities for tourism in the Caribbean region. He was able to acquire the land on which to build his hotels and resorts. Having acquired the land he was able to construct the physical capital (the building and equipment). In order to win loyal customers he then needed to employ top-quality labour to promote the image of his company. Using his entrepreneurial talent he has been able to make a profit for himself and other investors in his company, while at the same time paying attractive rewards (factor incomes) to the people who supplied his business with labour, capital and land.

Table 2.2.1 The rewards to factors of production

| Factor | Reward |
|--------|--------|
| Labour | Wages |
| Land | Rent |
| Capital | Interest |
| Enterprise | Profit |

### SUMMARY QUESTIONS

Which factor of production:

a earns rent

b organises other factors

c receives paid wages

d includes machines and tools

e would include natural resources

f is rewarded with profit?

# Land

Natural resources such as wind are classified as land

## What is land?

Economists use the term *land* to describe a range of natural resources. Land can be an area of ground that can be used for growing crops or building houses, but it also includes:

• fish in the sea, rivers or lakes
• sun and wind power that can be used for energy
• oil
• minerals such as copper and bauxite.

The main characteristic of land is that it is not man-made. It is a natural resource. The quantity of land available in an economy is not fixed. It can be increased, for example by reclaiming land from the sea, or by finding new reserves of oil and minerals.

## The productivity of land

The productivity of land is a measure of output that can be produced by a given unit. For example, the productivity of one hectare of land may be $10 000 worth of bananas in a year. Productivity of land can be measured in two ways:

• in terms of physical product – how many units of output the land will produce, for example 2000 pineapples
• in terms of revenue product – the value of the physical product when it is sold, for example $2000 worth of pineapples, assuming that each pineapple sells for $1.

The productivity of land can be increased by:

• altering its physical characteristics, for example by adding fertiliser
• combining the land with more advanced forms of other resources, for example harvesting sweet potatoes with a tractor rather than by hand with a pitchfork, which may lead to fewer damaged potatoes.

## Land and rent

Land is very important in economics because most, if not all, goods and services that society uses involve some natural resources. Early economists were particularly interested in land because it helped them to develop the important concept of **economic rent**. This refers to the surplus that the owner of a resource is able to get from the use of the resource. Look at the following example.

Ramesh has a field which he can use to grow either tomatoes or sweet potatoes. He will sell all of what he grows in the field at the local market. If he grows sweet potatoes he will earn $600 a year. If he grows tomatoes he will earn $1000 a year.

The surplus from growing tomatoes is thus $400 a year (Table 2.3.1):

**Table 2.3.1 Deriving economic rent as a surplus**

| $1000 Revenue from tomatoes | minus | $600 Potential revenue from sweet potatoes | equals | $400 Economic rent |
|---|---|---|---|---|

We can express this in another way (Table 2.3.2):

**Table 2.3.2 Economic rent as a surplus over and above opportunity cost**

| Revenue product from tomatoes | minus | Opportunity cost of revenue from sweet potatoes | equals | Economic rent |
|---|---|---|---|---|

When the early economists developed the idea of rent, many natural resources had no alternative economic uses. So if oil was discovered in a desert, there was no opportunity cost in using the land for oil production, as it would be unsuitable for anything else. All the revenue received from extracting the oil was thus a rent to the oil driller.

Today most natural resources can be used in a number of different ways, so there is an opportunity cost involved in the use of those resources. For example a piece of land could be used to build a supermarket, a dance and music club or a hotel, or it could be left as a nature reserve. The opportunity cost of using a particular area of land for a specific purpose is the next best use to which it could be put. What economists refer to as economic rent is the surplus over and above the opportunity cost.

**DID YOU KNOW?**

Any surplus over and above the opportunity cost of economic activity is 'economic rent'.

**SUMMARY QUESTIONS**

1 What will happen to the productivity of land when:

a it is irrigated

b it is damaged by a hurricane

c it is over-farmed

d fertiliser is added to it?

2 Why would solar power (energy from the sun) be classified as land?

3 What is the main difference between land and other factors of production?

**KEY POINTS**

- Rent is a surplus.
- Rent is a reward for the use of a natural resource.
- Rent is the surplus that the owner of the land receives over and above the opportunity cost of using that land in an alternative way.

# Labour

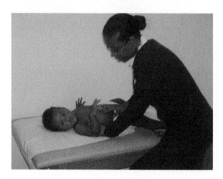

Skilled workers have extensive training and their productivity is high

## Definition of labour

Labour is the human energy and mental skills used to produce economic goods. For example, bricklayers use not only physical energy to lift and place bricks, but also their mental powers to decide where to place the bricks, how much cement to apply and how to tackle unusual surfaces and unpredictable events. Some jobs involve more physical labour, for example cutting sugar cane with a cutlass, while others focus more on mental skills, for example a lawyer arguing a case in a law court or a business manager making business plans.

### Skilled and unskilled labour

Economists distinguish between skilled and unskilled labour. Skilled labour is carried out by individuals who have developed their skills by practising and training over time. For example, they may have had an apprenticeship – a period of training in which to learn their skills. Unskilled work can be done with very little training (in some instances none at all).

A skilled worker can carry out more complicated and valuable tasks with little or no supervision. An unskilled worker can carry out routine tasks but may need a lot of supervision when carrying out new tasks.

### The productivity of labour

The productivity of labour refers to the output per worker per unit of time. For example, Michael Harrison, a mason, is able to lay 200 bricks in 4 hours. His productivity is 50 bricks per hour. Beverley Dean works in a factory tailoring shirts. She can produce 40 shirts in 8 hours. Her productivity is 5 shirts per hour.

The productivity of labour depends on:

- the quality of the other factors with which labour is working: workers using modern equipment will have a higher output per hour than those working with poor-quality equipment – so labour that is efficiently managed will be more productive than labour that is poorly managed
- the amount of training and skills that the labour has: the more highly trained and skilled the labour, the greater its productivity.

## Productivity at different levels of output

Labour is most productive when it is combined efficiently with other factors of production. A factory with too few labourers will have low levels of output per person. Productivity will increase if more labour is employed, for example because workers are able to specialise. However, if too many people are employed they will become inefficient, for example workers getting in each other's way. Economists use the law of increasing and diminishing returns to a factor of production to explain how productivity alters at different levels of output. When output is increased at low levels of output there will be increasing returns (increased productivity gains). Beyond a certain point, however, diminishing returns will set in (productivity losses). This can be illustrated in a productivity curve showing average productivity per employee at different levels of output (Figure 2.4.1).

**Figure 2.4.1** Increasing and decreasing productivity: the average productivity curve

## The supply of labour

The supply of labour means the quantity that is available at a particular moment in time. For example, if the government contractor is looking for labour to construct new government buildings, it will have to try to recruit from the existing supply of skilled and unskilled labour in the country. In this case this may include unskilled workers, for example labourers, and also skilled workers such as architects and engineers.

The more a country spends on education and training, the greater its supply of skilled labour.

The supply of labour in a country depends on the number of people in the country available for employment, that is those of working age who are willing and able to work. The supply of labour in particular industries and jobs depends on the number of people with the necessary skills and training.

**DID YOU KNOW?**

Where the supply of labour is limited this will help to push up wages because employers will have to compete with each other to employ scarce labour. For example, the wages of skilled information technology professionals are high, while basic manual labourers will receive much lower wages.

**KEY POINTS**

- Labour consists of physical and mental work.
- The supply of labour is determined by education and training.
- Skilled labour is more productive than unskilled labour.

**SUMMARY QUESTIONS**

1 Describe three ways in which the productivity of labour could be increased.

2 How might the supply of labour be increased?

Focusing on one or a small number of tasks increases productivity

## The division of labour

Specialisation occurs when an economic unit or individual – for example a factory or a factory worker – concentrates on a particular task. The division of labour is the specialisation of workers on given tasks and work roles. Today most people have a specialist job of work, whether this is as a builder, an office worker, a doctor or a teacher. These specialists may then employ other specialists to carry out work for them – to paint their house, to care for them when they are ill or to teach them a new skill.

Specialisation involves concentrating on a particular task. Division of labour involves specialisation by job task. Figure 2.5.1 shows some of the specialist tasks carried out in a modern factory producing bottled drinks.

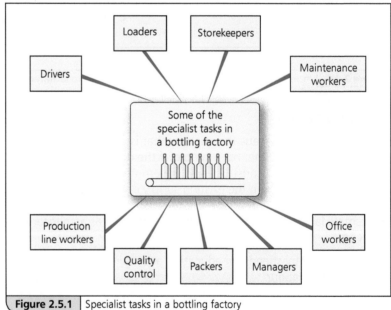

**Figure 2.5.1** Specialist tasks in a bottling factory

Each of these specialists concentrates on a particular task or job role. For example, a storekeeper is responsible for the materials, parts and other supplies that are received by the company. These need to be carefully checked, recorded and stored so that they are available as soon as they are required.

## Types of division of labour

There are three main types of division of labour:

**1** Division of labour within a factory or plant: individuals or groups of workers specialise in given tasks, as shown in Figure 2.5.1.

2  Geographical division of labour: within a country, labour specialises in particular areas. For example, in a capital city such as Port of Spain, many employees specialise in office and commercial work. In country areas more employees specialise in agriculture.

3  International division of labour: this is where labour in different countries specialises in different tasks. For example, in many cities in China, workers concentrate on manufacturing computers and other modern goods. In parts of Bangladesh and Pakistan, workers concentrate on making textile products.

## Advantages of the division of labour

Advantages from the division of labour provide benefits for individuals, the organisations that they work for and the economy as a whole. For example:

- Increase in skill: by doing something repeatedly the employee becomes more skilled. A skilled worker is more productive than an unskilled one.
- Time saving: it takes time to change from one task to another. Specialisation helps to eliminate wasted time.
- Specialisation in 'best lines': division of labour makes it possible for people to concentrate on what they do best. Some people like working with their hands, others enjoy selling things.
- Use of supporting technology: specialists can use technical equipment that makes their work easier and enhances their skills. Most specialist work is supported by specialist machinery.
- Higher earnings: a specialist can usually earn more than a non-specialist.

## Disadvantages of the division of labour

There are a number of disadvantages to the division of labour:

- Dependency: because of specialisation, many individuals and processes become dependent on each other. If the person or machine at the previous stage to you is slow, unreliable or inefficient, your own work may suffer.
- Unemployment: specialisation in a specific task or job can be harmful if the economy no longer needs that specialism.
- Boredom: if the work is repetitive and not challenging, workers can become bored. This leads to accidents and low job satisfaction.
- Over-concentration: by concentrating on specialist skills, individuals may not develop their other abilities. If they concentrate on a job that lots of other people do, their wages may be low.

**KEY POINTS**

- Specialisation of individuals at work is called the division of labour.
- Division of labour enables individuals to become more skilled and more productive.

**SUMMARY QUESTIONS**

1  Define the term 'division of labour'.

2  List four advantages of the division of labour for:

a  producers

b  employees

c  the economy.

# Capital

## What is capital?

Economists use the term *capital* to refer to real assets that are used in the production of goods and services. A **real asset** is also referred to as a **fixed asset**. This relates to items that help an economic unit, such as a business, to generate earnings over a period of time. Real assets are therefore items such as factory buildings, machinery and equipment. Capital can be used to make consumer goods, for example bread, CD players, and other capital goods, for example tractors, factory machines. Capital items tend to be durable – that is, they last a long time. Another feature of a capital item is that it is likely to be expensive, for example a taxi cab or agricultural machinery can cost thousands of dollars.

| CASE STUDY | Sabina Park |
| --- | --- |

The George Headley Stand represents a fine investment in capital

Sabina Park in Kingston, Jamaica is one of the most famous cricket grounds in the world, with the Blue Mountains forming a magnificent backdrop. It is a modern cricket ground built to take thousands of spectators who are able to view top-class regional matches and test matches between the West Indies and other cricket-playing nations. Spectators enter the ground through turnstiles and there are floodlights for night-time cricket.

The George Headley Stand for spectators is the most familiar, but there are many other facilities such as private boxes and a members' stand. The ground comes with other facilities too, such as restaurants and pitch-side facilities such as a site screen, covers for the pitch in wet weather and modern rolling and grass-cutting equipment.

### Questions

**1** From the case study identify at least six items of capital which are the real assets of Sabina Park cricket ground.

**2** How do these assets enable the cricket authorities to generate revenue over time?

**3** What actions could the owners of Sabina Park cricket ground take to improve the capital available to them?

## The accumulation of capital

Capital is accumulated over time through a process known as investment. For example, when Sabina Park became a test cricket ground in the 1930s, most of the spectators would have stood, or sat on mounds overlooking the ground. Today the ground holds 30 000 spectators in seated stands. Year by year the owners have been able to improve the facilities by a process of investment in new capital. One such facility is the George Headley Stand which was built with a capacity of 8000 spectators. The development of floodlights at the ground extended the hours for which matches can take place, so increasing the productivity of the ground. (Look back to 1.1 for discussion of investment.)

Capital is often acquired by borrowing money to finance a project. For example, a company may borrow $10 000 from the bank to buy a new piece of machinery. It will then pay the bank back with regular interest payments in addition to the repayment of the sum initially borrowed.

## Capital and labour-intensive industries

Some industries are labour-intensive. This means that they employ a lot of labour relative to the amount of capital.

Some industries are capital-intensive. This means that they employ a lot of capital relative to the amount of labour.

Over time most industries become more capital-intensive. For example, traditionally agriculture was a labour-intensive industry. With the development of agricultural machinery such as tractors, agriculture has become more capital-intensive and fewer people are employed per hectare of land. Similarly in factory production, a car production line used to involve many workers as well as machinery. Over time, automatic machinery has replaced many of the workers. Some car production lines are now operated almost entirely by factory robots.

Although manufacturing has become more and more capital-intensive, some personal service industries, for example hairdressing and dentistry, are more labour-intensive (Figure 2.6.1).

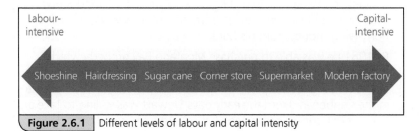

| **Figure 2.6.1** | Different levels of labour and capital intensity |

# Entrepreneurial talent

Candidates should be able to:

• describe entrepreneurial talent.

**DID YOU KNOW?**

Drilling for oil is risky: exploring for new fields in difficult geographical terrain, for example under the ice caps or at great depths under the ocean, is highly risky but can lead to multi-billion-dollar finds.

**EXAM TIP**

Later in this book you will be introduced to the concept of normal profit. This refers to the minimum amount of profit required to encourage an entrepreneur to stay in a particular line of business. It is the opportunity cost to the entrepreneur of providing their enterpreneurial flair to a particular enterprise. Of course most entrepreneurs receive more than 'normal profit'. Profit that is greater than normal profit is termed 'abnormal profit'.

## Who are entrepreneurs?

Entrepreneurs are people prepared to take risks to achieve rewards, mainly in the form of profit. The profit an entrepreneur makes is the difference between the revenue (money receipts from sales) and the costs of production (money paid for the use of other factors of production, for example wages for labour). The total profit that a business will make for supplying a given quantity of output to the market is calculated by deducting total costs from total revenue.

Total revenue − Total cost = Total profit

The case study that follows gives a brief account of the enterprising activities of a successful entrepreneur.

| **CASE STUDY** | Gordon Butch Stewart |
| --- | --- |

Butch Stewart took a risk in setting up the Sandals Resort chain

Gordon Butch Stewart is a Jamaican entrepreneur who founded Sandals and Beaches Family Resorts. Today he is the owner of a billion-dollar business based in Jamaica. This includes 18 Caribbean resorts and the *Jamaica Observer* newspaper. He also owns a range of other enterprises, and his group of companies is Jamaica's biggest foreign currency earner.

Gordon Butch Stewart started out as a sales manager for the Curaçao Trading Company before setting up, in 1968, his first business, Appliance Trader Ltd, focusing on air conditioning. This business grew rapidly. In setting up Appliance Trader Ltd Stewart used some of his own savings from his previous work, as well as borrowing money from his bank.

By 1981 he was able to purchase Montego Bay property which formed the basis for his Sandals Resorts chain: a seaside hotel resort catering for couples. Today he employs nearly 10 000 people in the Caribbean. From the early days Stewart was willing to take a risk. His enterprises combined all the factors of production – labour (for example resort employees), land (on which the resorts were built), capital (the real assets such as hotel buildings) and of course his own enterprise. Stewart believes that to operate in business you have to be willing to take calculated risks.

## Questions

1 How did Gordon Butch Stewart take a risk when he set up Appliance Trader Ltd?

2 How might Gordon Butch Stewart have lost out and how could he have gained from the venture?

3 Explain how purchasing Montego Bay property was also an entrepreneurial activity.

4 Why does Gordon Butch Stewart require other factors of production?

Setting up the Sandals Resorts chain illustrates the enterprise of Gordon Butch Stewart. He came up with an idea that he was willing to back with his own time, effort and money. Although he would have made detailed plans, there was no guarantee that the business would succeed. At the time it would have been considered a highly risky venture.

Typically in business there is a direct relationship between risk and reward. The bigger the risk, the greater the possible rewards, but also the greater the possible losses. This is illustrated in Figure 2.7.1.

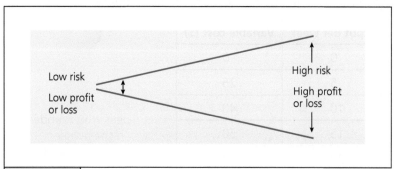

**Figure 2.7.1** | The relationship between risk and reward

Taking a high risk can lead to such disastrous losses that business entrepreneurs have to sell all of their possessions to cover the loss. However, should the risk pay off then the rewards can be very high, as they have been for Gordon Butch Stewart.

## SUMMARY QUESTIONS

1 Why do entrepreneurs take risks?

2 What is the relationship between risk and possible return?

# The costs of production 1: fixed and variable costs

Candidates should be able to:

- identify the costs associated with production – fixed and variable costs.

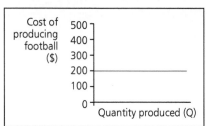

| Figure 2.8.1 | Fixed costs of producing footballs |

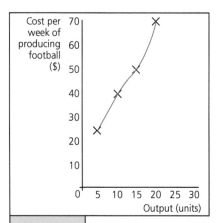

| Figure 2.8.2 | The variable cost to a firm of producing different quantities of footballs |

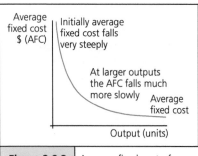

| Figure 2.8.3 | Average fixed cost of increasing output |

## Costs

Producing goods costs money. A business enterprise, for example, needs to buy raw materials, pay wages and spend money on marketing the finished product. Economists divide the cost of production into two main types:

- **Fixed costs** do not alter with the quantity of output.
- **Variable costs** increase directly as output increases.

### Fixed costs

Fixed costs are costs that have to be paid whether the business is producing nothing or thousands of units. They depend on the type of business, but often include items such as rent and rates, interest on money borrowed and wages, which are not related to how much is produced. Fixed costs can be illustrated as a horizontal straight line: Figure 2.8.1 shows that the costs of a small firm producing footballs are $200 a week, whether it produces no balls, 5 balls or 25 balls.

### Variable costs

Variable costs, such as the cost of raw materials, are zero when output is zero and rise directly with output. The table shows the variable costs of the football-manufacturing company.

| Output per week | Variable cost ($) |
|:---:|:---:|
| 0 | 0 |
| 5 | 25 |
| 10 | 40 |
| 15 | 50 |
| 20 | 70 |

Figure 2.8.2 shows the variable costs of producing different quantities of footballs as a graph.

### Average fixed cost

The greater the number of goods produced, the more the fixed costs will be spread over the output. If a bottling plant produces only 100 bottles a week, each bottle produced would involve a very high fixed cost element. In practice, bottling plants produce tens of thousands of bottles a week and the total fixed cost is spread over a large output (resulting in a low average cost per unit).

Figure 2.8.3 shows the **average fixed cost** (AFC) as output increases. As the level of output increases, the fixed cost per unit falls.

## Average variable cost

Variable costs of production usually include the raw materials and increases in labour to produce more goods, and **average variable costs** (AVC) alter as output increases. For example, a business with a small output will not be able to make good use of variable resources. Two or three workers in a bottling factory would not be enough to handle the machinery efficiently, but a higher number would mean that they could be organised so that each additional worker added to production at an increasing rate. For example, each worker could specialise in a small number of tasks.

However, the increase in production cannot keep accelerating (because the equipment and factory floor capacity is limited). Additional labourers would start to get in each other's way and thus work less efficiently, and the average variable cost of producing more would start to rise.

Figure 2.8.4 shows the average variable cost as a curve that falls at first and later starts to rise.

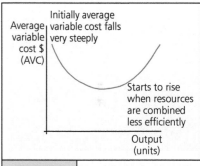

**Figure 2.8.4** | Average variable cost

---

**CASE STUDY** | Costs at different levels of output

A business has fixed costs of $1000 a week. Variable costs at different levels of output are shown in the table.

| Output | Average variable cost per unit |
|--------|-------------------------------|
| 100 | 10 cents |
| 200 | 8 cents |
| 300 | 6 cents |
| 400 | 8 cents |
| 500 | 10 cents |

### Questions

1 Illustrate the average variable cost curve on a graph.

2 Explain why it has the shape that it does.

3 Calculate the average fixed cost at each of the levels of output shown in the table.

4 Draw and then explain the shape of the average fixed cost curve.

---

---

### SUMMARY QUESTION

If it costs $100 to produce 0 units, $110 to produce 10 units, and $120 to produce 20 units:

a What is the fixed cost of production?

b What do variable costs vary with?

# The costs of production 2: output and costs

Candidates should be able to:

- identify the costs associated with production – total and average costs.

By working out the cost of producing items such as footballs, Nike is able to decide on suitable prices to charge to cover costs and make a profit

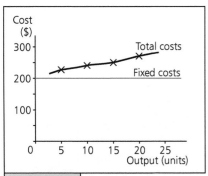

**Figure 2.9.1** | Fixed and total costs

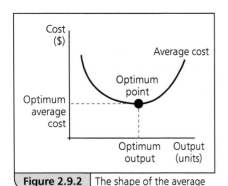

**Figure 2.9.2** | The shape of the average cost curve

## Total cost

**Total cost** can be calculated by adding the fixed and variable costs at different levels of output. Figure 2.9.1 shows in graph form the total, fixed and variable costs given in the table below. The shape of the total costs curve makes sense if you think that the more goods produced, the higher the overall cost of producing them.

| Output per week | Fixed cost ($) | Variable cost ($) | Total cost ($) |
|---|---|---|---|
| 0 | 200 | 0 | 200 |
| 5 | 200 | 25 | 225 |
| 10 | 200 | 40 | 240 |
| 15 | 200 | 50 | 250 |
| 20 | 200 | 70 | 270 |

## Average cost

**Average cost** is the cost of producing a unit of product at a particular output.

To calculate average cost, use the following formula:

$$\text{Average cost} = \frac{\text{Total cost}}{\text{Output}}$$

For example, in the table above, the average cost of producing 10 products would be $24 (240/10). The average cost of producing 20 products would be $13.50 (270/20).

### The shape of the average cost curve

It is important to know and understand the shape of a typical average cost curve. Figure 2.9.2 shows its characteristic U-shape.

It has this shape because:

1 Average fixed cost is falling as output levels increase. This effect pulls the curve down at a slower and slower rate. So if fixed costs are $1000, producing two units rather than one will lower the curve from $1000 to produce 1 unit, to $500 to produce 2 units. However, at much higher levels of output, for example producing 1000 units rather than 999, you will only be reducing the average fixed cost from $1.11 to $1.00 – that is, by just a few cents.

2 Average variable cost falls initially as the firm is able to combine its factors of production more efficiently. However, there comes a point at which inefficiencies creep into the production plant.

The lowest point on the average cost curve shows the point at which the business is combining its resources most efficiently. We call this lowest point the **optimum output** level.

## Marginal costs

Economists also place great emphasis on the **marginal cost of production**, the additional cost of producing one additional unit of output. For example, if the total cost of producing 100 units of a good is $1000 and the total cost of producing 101 units is $1009, then the marginal cost of producing the 101st unit is $9. The importance of knowing the marginal cost is that when marginal costs are lower than marginal revenues (the extra receipt from producing the additional unit), it will be worth expanding production.

---

**CASE STUDY** | Calculating average cost

A firm has calculated that its total costs (fixed + variable costs) at different levels of daily output are as follows:

| Output per day | Total cost ($) | Average cost ($) |
|---|---|---|
| 0 | 10.00 | |
| 1 | 15.00 | |
| 2 | 18.00 | |
| 3 | 20.00 | |
| 4 | 21.00 | |
| 5 | 23.00 | |
| 6 | 26.00 | |
| 7 | 30.00 | |
| 8 | 35.00 | |
| 9 | 41.00 | |

### Questions

**1** Copy the table. Using the data given, calculate the average cost of production for a firm at different output levels, and complete the final column for each level.

**2** At what point does average cost start to rise?

**3** Explain why average cost starts to rise at this point.

**Table 2.9.1** Some useful definitions of costs

| | |
|---|---|
| Total fixed cost | The sum of all of the different types of fixed costs at different outputs |
| Total variable cost | The sum of all of the variable costs at different outputs |
| Total cost | The sum of total fixed cost and total variable cost at different outputs |
| Average fixed cost | The total fixed cost divided by the level of output |
| Average variable cost | The total variable cost divided by the level of output |
| Average total cost | The total cost divided by the level of output |

# Short-run and long-run costs

It takes time to build a factory (the long period)

## Time periods

Economists make an important distinction between the short term and the long term. In the short term an organisation has available a set quantity of fixed factors of production; it cannot change the quantity of fixed capital. For example, a factory that produces men's shirts may be a small building with five machines. It would take time for the business to build a larger factory and buy additional machines.

The long period is the period in which the quantity and/or quality of fixed assets available to the company can be increased.

## Short-run costs

In the short run the shape of the average cost curve is determined by the rules set out in 2.9. The average cost curve has a characteristic U-shape, showing that initially average costs fall as output is increased with a given quantity of fixed factors of production. Beyond the optimum point, production becomes less efficient as more variable factors are combined with fixed factors.

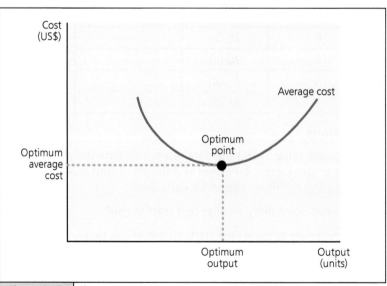

**Figure 2.10.1** Short-run costs

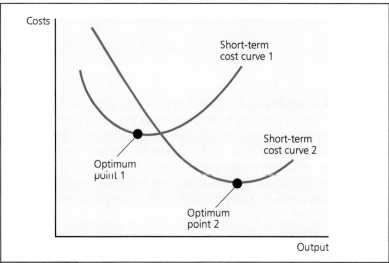

**Figure 2.10.2** The optimum output as a firm grows

## Long-run costs

In the long period more fixed factors can be employed, for example a larger, more modern factory and more efficient machines that can produce larger quantities more cheaply.

Figure 2.10.2 contrasts two situations to show how in the long run average costs of production fall.

In the first situation (curve 1) the company produces on a relatively small scale. The fixed cost of building a factory and installing machinery is relatively low. In the second situation (curve 2) the company produces on a larger scale. The fixed cost of building the factory and installing the machinery is relatively high.

If we compare the average cost of the two companies, we can see that:

• the average cost curve for the company when it is small starts at a lower point than when the firm becomes larger (because fixed costs are lower)

• the optimum point on the average cost curve is lower for the firm when it becomes larger; because the firm employs larger, more advanced units of capital it is able to spread the fixed costs of production over a larger output.

A long-run average cost curve shows the cost per unit of output in the long run. All points on the line represent least cost factor combinations.

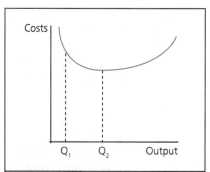

**Figure 2.10.3** A long-run average cost curve

**SUMMARY QUESTIONS**

1 In economic terms, how long is the short period?

2 What shape is the average cost curve? Why does it have this shape?

# Economies of scale

Large-scale production enables low-cost production

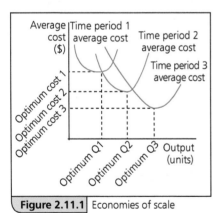

**Figure 2.11.1** Economies of scale

**Economies of scale** are the advantages of producing on a scale large enough for a business to be able to cut the cost of individual units of production. Economies of scale enable a business to reduce its average cost curve. Figure 2.11.1 shows the average cost for a growing business in three successive time periods. In period 2 it can produce a larger output at a lower average cost than in period 1. In period 3 it can produce a larger output at a lower average cost than in period 2.

Businesses can benefit from two main types of economies of scale: internal and external. Internal economies are the advantages that a firm gains from its own growth. They include technical, marketing, financial and risk-bearing economies of scale. External economies are the advantages gained from the growth and improvement of a firm's industry and locality.

## Internal economies of scale

### Technical economies of scale

Large firms can benefit from better techniques of production. For example, automated plant and equipment (such as in a bottling plant) may be so expensive to install that only large companies can afford it. Automated production lines enable very high production at low unit cost and can be run 24 hours a day, 7 days a week. One worker working on their own with a cutlass in a sugar cane field is much less efficient than the same worker operating with mechanised cutting equipment in a much larger field.

### Marketing economies of scale

**Marketing economies** relate to operating in the market place for buying and selling goods. Large firms are able to buy and sell in bulk, and obtain discounts when they do this. When they sell in bulk this cuts down the distribution costs as they avoid the costs of supplying many separate outlets. The cost of creating a global advertising campaign can be spread over the billions of people who watch the television advertisement across the globe.

### Financial economies of scale

Large firms usually find it easier and cheaper to borrow money. A huge multinational like the international brewery company Diageo is able to borrow large amounts of money to finance its activities. The company was able to borrow cheaply from banks to purchase the famous Jamaican Red Stripe beer brand. This was originally produced by the Jamaican company Desnoes and Geddes.

### Risk-bearing economies of scale

Large firms can spread their risks in several ways:

- Product diversification: producing and selling many different products.
- Market diversification: producing and selling in many different countries and regions.
- Supplier diversification: using several different suppliers in case one is unable to supply on time.
- Production diversification: having several different production plants.

## External economies of scale

Whereas internal economies relate to the growth of a single firm, external economies of scale relate to the growth of an industry. External economies of scale will benefit most or all the firms in an industry. For example, the development of an international airport in Barbados benefits all the businesses in the tourist industry, such as taxi firms, hotels and restaurants. The development of Barbados as a centre of excellence for IT research benefits all the companies in the IT industry. The existence of a campus of the University of the West Indies in Barbados provides all businesses there with a supply of well-qualified graduates.

---

**CASE STUDY** | Internal and external economies

Leroy is considering setting up a large IT business to produce websites for companies in Jamaica. He has made a list of the advantages of setting up a large rather than a smaller business, which he is going to present to his bank manager.

### Questions

Which of the following advantages should be classified as internal economies and which as external economies? In each case explain why.

1 There has been a growth in the number of people with IT qualifications in Jamaica.

2 He would be able to borrow more cheaply than if he set up as a small business.

3 Jamaica has been developing a reputation as a specialist provider of IT services.

4 He would be able to afford to invest in more sophisticated IT systems.

5 He would be able to spread his risks by providing websites to more IT businesses.

6 The University of the West Indies is providing advice and guidance to new IT entrepreneurs as the sector grows in the Caribbean.

**SUMMARY QUESTIONS**

1 Is it possible for all firms to benefit from economies of scale?

2 If a firm doubles in size, does it benefit from internal or external economies? Give a reason for your answer.

# Diseconomies of scale

## What are diseconomies?

Diseconomies arise when a firm becomes too large and the production of additional units leads to an increase in costs. A firm may face a number of problems as a result of growing too large. Typical problems include:

• Communication problems: Decisions that managers and other decision-makers try to make may be poorly understood, leading to mistakes and errors, with a negative impact on productivity.

• Control problems: As the firm becomes larger it may be difficult for managers and supervisors to control what is going on in the organisation. Management can become more complex and additional layers of management are required. Creating too many management levels can be costly and can lead to poor communication.

• Industrial problems: In large companies there may be poorer relations between managers, supervisors and employees, leading to more disputes, strikes by workers and other actions that reduce productivity.

As a result, as a firm becomes larger, the long-term average cost curve might start to rise beyond a certain size of output. Rising long-term average costs would illustrate the impact of diseconomies of scale.

### CASE STUDY | *Freedom of the Seas*

Managing a large ship such as *Freedom of the Seas* is a complex operation

The *Freedom of the Seas* is one of the world's largest cruise ships, regularly touring territories in the Caribbean. The ship has 1800 rooms and can carry up to 5000 passengers and crew.

This ship illustrates many of the advantages of economies of scale, in particular technical economies. As a large ship it is able to offer many more facilities than smaller cruise vessels. In addition the cost of building and fitting out the ship was much lower relative to each passenger who can be carried than for a smaller ship. To build a small ship requires much less metal per passenger carried than a larger ship, but the capacity of the ship rises much faster than the increase in the quantity of metal used in its construction.

However, there are also some diseconomies that come with scale:

- A marketing diseconomy of scale may be that while it is easy to advertise to attract passengers to fill a small cruise liner, much larger expenditures may be needed to fill a larger one. There is also a risk of some of the berths on the ship remaining unsold and the liner sailing short of capacity. Even if 900 rooms are filled rather than 1800, the same bills for crew and fuel still have to be paid.

- Managing and organising a large ship with so many passengers may be much more difficult. If it is too large to manage efficiently, this may lead to complaints and the need to pay refunds and compensation.

- There could also be financial diseconomies. A small ocean liner might be bought by a company without having to borrow finance. A larger liner might require a lot of borrowing, and consequently a lot of interest needing to be paid.

### Questions

1 Make a list of economies of scale from building and operating a large ocean liner. List them as technical, marketing, financial and risk spreading.

2 For each of the economies of scale listed try to identify a possible diseconomy of scale.

## When do diseconomies set in?

The point at which diseconomies of scale start to set in for a business will vary from industry to industry. Many manufacturing activities, for example bottling and canning, benefit from large-scale economies. However, some goods and services – dentistry, hairdressing, and massage, for example – require a lot of attention to detail, so diseconomies are likely to arise at much lower outputs. This is why in the service industry there are many small rather than large businesses.

Entrepreneurs must be careful not to allow diseconomies to set into their business. Often diseconomies result from being overambitious and spreading resources too thinly rather than concentrating on one area. If a firm becomes too large it should consider selling off parts of the business, particularly those parts that are not at the core of the business.

**EXAM TIP**

The ability of a firm to benefit from economies of scale typically depends on:

- the size of the market
- the share of the market that the firm has
- how well organised the firm is.

Where there is only a small market and/ or the firm only has a small share, it will have far fewer opportunities to take advantage of economies of scale.

### KEY POINTS

- A diseconomy of scale is a disadvantage to a firm that results from the growth of the firm.

- Diseconomies set in when a firm grows too large, leading to rising unit costs of production.

### SUMMARY QUESTIONS

1 Give an example of an external diseconomy of scale.

2 What effect does this diseconomy have on average costs? Illustrate your answer.

# Economic systems

In a planned economy like that of Cuba the government makes many economic decisions

## Alternative systems

In 1.2 we defined the economy as a system that creates wealth. There are a number of alternative ways of organising this system (Figure 2.13.1).

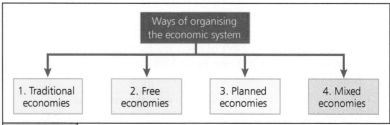

**Figure 2.13.1** Organising the economic system

In 2.13 the first three economies are considered. The mixed economy (a combination of 1, 2 and 3) is looked at in 2.14.

## Resource allocation

The main problem facing an economic system is how to allocate scarce resources between the alternative purposes for which they can be used (Figure 2.13.2).

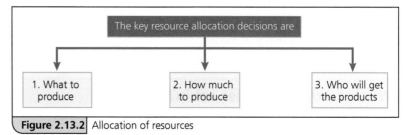

**Figure 2.13.2** Allocation of resources

## Traditional economies

A traditional economy is an area in which people engage in subsistence farming. Working on smallholdings of land, people produce enough for their own household consumption and perhaps trade a small surplus. Many Caribbean economies have such areas. The key decisions are:

- What to produce: products for sustenance – food crops, livestock.
- How much to produce: enough to live off and a small surplus to trade.
- Who will get the products: the smallholder and their family.

In a subsistence economy there is frequent bartering. This involves exchanging one good for another, for example six eggs for two plantains, rather than using money.

## Planned economies

Cuba is an example of a planned economy. Although changes are taking place there, the government owns many of the industries and land, and makes many of the decisions about what will be produced. The advantage of this system is that the government is able to make decisions to benefit everyone rather than just those who have the most money. The government is also able to guarantee jobs, although wages may be low. The government also provides important services such as health and education free to its citizens.

In this case the key decisions are:

- What to produce: goods and services that the government decides are needed by citizens.
- How much to produce: enough to meet the basic needs of all the people and enough extra to provide a good standard of life.
- Who gets the products: the products are shared out among citizens, so that even the weakest members of society, for example the elderly or people who are unable to work, get a reasonable share.

## Free or capitalist system

In a free market or capitalist system individuals set up their own enterprises to produce goods and services. Barbados is an economy operating largely on free enterprise lines. The advantage of this system is that individuals are free to choose what they want to purchase, and can spend their own money to gain maximum advantage for themselves. Land and businesses are privately owned rather than being owned by the government. The key decisions in this system are:

- What to produce: determined by independent businesses that seek to make a profit from producing the goods that consumers are prepared to purchase.
- How much to produce: businesses seek to produce levels of output that will maximise their profits; customers signal to businesses which products they want by showing that they are willing to pay the current market price.
- Who gets the products: consumers are able to acquire products by their purchases (some people think this is unfair, as it favours those with the highest incomes who can buy the most desirable products).

**Table 2.13.1** Planned and free economies

|  | Planned economy | Capitalist economy |
|---|---|---|
| Who makes economic decisions? | Mainly government planners | Consumers and producers |
| What/who determines what will be produced? | Government plans | The market (demand and supply) |
| How are goods produced? | Mainly by state-run industries | By private companies seeking profits |
| How are goods allocated in society? | By the state | Individuals choose what to buy with their incomes |

**SUMMARY QUESTIONS**

1 What type of economic system is there in your territory?

2 What are the main resource allocation decisions that have to be made in your economy?

3 Who makes these decisions?

# The mixed economy

In Antigua and Barbuda some hotels are owned by the government

## Mixed economies

A **mixed economy** combines elements of a market economy with some government interference, such as some ownership of businesses (Figure 2.14.1).

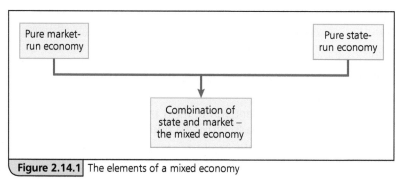

**Figure 2.14.1** The elements of a mixed economy

| CASE STUDY | Antigua and Barbuda: a mixed economy |
| --- | --- |

In Antigua and Barbuda tourism accounts for over 50 per cent of employment and income. The construction industry is also a major employer as a result of its close association with building new tourist complexes and hotels. Agriculture, including the manufacture of sea island cotton, is also important to the island economy. The fishing industry is a relatively small employer.

The tourism industry tends to be dominated by foreign capital. The government in Antigua and Barbuda has taken a number of steps to make sure that the economy is not over-reliant on foreign capital. From the 1980s onwards the government invested in electric power, seaports, airports, water supply, energy and telecommunications. It also invested in the tourism industry to provide an example to privately owned hotel and resort companies. The government kept its hotels open all year round to make sure that people working in this sector had employment for 12 months a year. This encouraged private firms to follow suit.

The government of Antigua and Barbuda has also encouraged foreign investment in manufacturing industry by building factories and other industrial plant to encourage companies to take over these ready-made facilities. Industries include processors of local agricultural products as well as furniture manufacturing and clothing industries.

## Questions

**1** Give four examples of industries with privately owned companies in Antigua and Barbuda.

**2** Give three examples of industries in which there is government intervention that provides basic infrastructure for the people of Antigua and Barbuda.

**3** Give three examples of other industries in which the government intervenes to provide employment in Antigua and Barbuda.

## Characteristics of a mixed economy

The following are the key characteristics of a mixed economy:

- Some productive resources are owned by the government and some by private companies and individuals. For example, in many countries the government owns roads, railways, airports and ports. It may also own the electricity, gas and water companies and the resources that come with them, such as pipelines and employees. The private sector (non-government owned) owns other resources such as beaches (hotels), land (agriculture) and shops (retail).

- The government may acquire enterprises from private sector businesses in order to run them itself. This may be to guarantee employment or to influence what is produced in the economy.

- In a mixed economy the government influences private sector decision-making, for example by subsidising private businesses to carry out certain activities such as growing some agricultural products or investing in green technology.

In a mixed economy the following decisions are made that relate to the use of resources:

- What to produce: some decisions are made by the government, others by private businesses. Consumers signal to businesses what goods they would like to be produced through their willingness to make purchases at the market price. Governments provide additional goods and services through state-owned enterprises, for example medical care and other essential services. In some countries the government runs industries of national importance, such as energy supply.

- How much to produce: the government decides how much of the goods that it produces will be supplied to market. In the production of schools it can determine how many children will go to school, or how much will be produced in government-owned businesses. Private industry will typically make many of the production decisions in a mixed economy in the same manner as in a free enterprise economy.

- Who gets the products: the government can decide who will get goods which it supplies itself. For example, it may decide that all children will go to school, or that government hotels will be open all year. When these decisions are made by private businesses they are based on price and costs of production.

### EXAM TIP

Make it clear in answering questions about rent that this is not simply a reward to owners of physical land. It is also a reward to suppliers of other natural resources, for example oil, gas and minerals.

### KEY POINTS

- The mixed economy combines planned and free market economies.
- Most economies are mixed economies.
- In a mixed economy some decisions are made by the government and some by firms and households.

### SUMMARY QUESTION

Give examples of decision-makers in a mixed economy.

# The merits and demerits of different systems

In a market or mixed economy there are many small entrepreneurs running their own businesses

## Assessing the merits of different systems

As we have seen, there are four types of economic system:

- the traditional economy
- the market economy
- the planned economy
- the mixed economy.

The merits of each system can be assessed in terms of:

- efficiency in allocating scarce resources
- providing goods and services to each sector of the population: rich, middle and low income.

An example of each, with its merits and demerits, is given below.

### The traditional economy

- Example: a hunter-gatherer society or a remote agricultural community.
- Merits: members of society cooperate to produce goods and exchange items through barter. The needs of low-income households are looked after by group activity.
- Demerits: typically the society operates at a subsistence level, so most households fit into the low-income group. Little surplus to trade is produced.

### The market economy

- Example: a society in which there is no government sector. The USA is seen as the closest example of this type of economy.
- Merits: individual economic units – businesses and consumers – are free to choose what they produce or buy, and what prices they will charge. Because people are working for themselves they tend to work hard. A market economy is an efficient way of channelling resources into types of production in which consumers express an interest.
- Demerits: benefits favour those with capital (rich and middle-income sectors of society); the system disadvantages low-income households. A weakness of the market economy is that decisions about production often ignore environmental effects. In the pursuit of profit, entrepreneurs may pollute the environment. Consumers may also purchase goods that have a harmful effect on the environment, for example by smoking cigarettes and using products that pollute, such as petrol.

## The planned economy

- Example: a society in which the government dominates the economy, for example Cuba. Government planners decide what will be produced, when and how.

- Merits: the government is able to secure a minimum standard of living for everyone. This is an advantage for low-income households. Resources managed and controlled by central planners enable economies of scale.

- Demerits: middle- and high-income households may feel restricted because they are not able to set up their own businesses and take risks related to reward. Government officials may be reluctant to take risks. While unemployment is eliminated, resources may be underemployed, with people working well below their potential. The planned economy may also fail to take account of impacts on the environment. In the rush for economic growth, some planned economies have created high levels of pollution.

## The mixed economy

- Examples: most Caribbean economies. The degree of the mix will depend on the current government in power and their particular ideology. Some have minimal government interference, others have a little more.

- Merits: combines the strength of the market and the planned economy. The market can make decisions where government decision-making is inappropriate, for example the operation of small shops. The government can make decisions where efficient supply is important, for example on road transport or the management of ports. The government can also provide for welfare needs. The mixed economy caters for the needs of high-, middle- and low-income members of society by allowing individual enterprise while at the same time providing a safety net for the poorest members of society.

- Demerits: combines the weaknesses of the market and the planned economy. Too much government interference can discourage effort and risk-taking; the bigger the state sector, the less opportunity there is for private business. Businesses and high- and middle-income households may be discouraged by the government taxing their profits and income to provide services free to the whole population.

Table 2.15.1 Traditional and mixed economies

|  | Traditional economy | Mixed economy |
|---|---|---|
| Who makes economic decisions? | Individual members of traditional society | Combination of the state (government) and private consumers and suppliers |
| What/who determines what will be produced? | Smallholders who focus on producing subsistence crops and implements | Combination of the state and the market |
| How are goods produced? | Using simple subsistence techniques | Combination of state-run and private businesses |
| How are goods allocated in society? | Smallholders get what they produce themselves and barter some items | Some goods and services allocated by the state (e.g. healthcare and public education), other goods and services bought privately |

### SUMMARY QUESTION

What arguments would you put forward to support the following ideas?

a A planned economy is better than a mixed economy.

b A mixed economy is better than a planned economy.

### KEY POINTS

- Each type of economic system has merits and demerits.

- Merits relate to how effective a system is in allocating resources and meeting the needs of low-, middle- and high-income earners.

- Most countries operate a mixed system based on some market activity supported by government intervention in the economy.

# Types of business organisation

## Types of business organisation in the market

There are five main types of business organisation in the free market. These are outlined below.

### The sole trader

As its name implies, the sole trader is a one-owner business. For example, many people in the Caribbean operate their own taxi business. They simply need a suitable vehicle, a driving permit and a private hire car licence. Other individuals operate as roadside food vendors, stall holders or plumbers; they fish and sell their catch or make and sell clothes, or run other similar businesses on their own. The benefit is that the business is easy to set up and they take all the profit themselves. Sole traders make all their own decisions and do not require a lot of capital. Note, however, that they may employ others to work for them. Disadvantages of being a sole trader include carrying all the responsibilities and work of the business, and having only limited capital.

Many taxi drivers operate as sole traders, others work for a larger company

### Partnerships

A partnership consists of two or more owners. It is set up with the creation of a **deed of partnership** lodged with a solicitor. This sets out responsibilities and payments and how profits and losses will be shared. Advantages of partnerships are that the owners share the workload (including hours worked), and that the partners bring more skills and capital to the business.

Partnerships are often found in professions, for example accountants, solicitors, dentists and doctors. They are also found in trades, for example building, plumbing and house decorating. As for sole traders, a disadvantage for partners is the lack of legal protection of limited liability. Owners of both these types of business are liable for the debts of their business and may have to sell personal possessions to meet them.

## Public and private companies

A company is a body that has been set up by following established legal guidelines (stating how it should operate) and is owned by shareholders. The company needs to be registered with a Registrar of Companies. Shareholders choose a Board of Directors to oversee the running of the business. The Board of Directors appoints managers to oversee the planning and day-to-day running of the business.

A company has limited liability. This means that if it has financial difficulties and has to repay debtors, the maximum amount that shareholders will have to pay to meet these debts is the value of their shares in the company.

There are two types of company: private and public. Private limited companies tend to be smaller and are often family businesses. There must be at least two shareholders. Shares in private companies are not traded on stock exchanges, and can usually be bought only with the permission of the board. Private companies can raise more capital than unlimited businesses by issuing shares, but not usually as much as public companies.

A public company has shares traded on one or more national stock exchanges. Large sums of capital can be raised quite quickly. The main benefit of being a public company is that it enables a business to acquire money to invest by attracting finance from people who are willing to buy shares.

Disadvantages of setting up companies are the amount of paperwork that must be dealt with, and the detailed records that are required by law. These include carefully audited accounts. Shares can be bought up by individuals and groups that want to take over the business and the original owners may lose control of their business.

## Cooperatives

'Cooperation' means working together in agreement. In a cooperative people join together to make decisions, work and share profits. Cooperators benefit from sharing responsibility and from pooling money and other resources. The cooperators, or members, are also the owners of the business, who share the rewards and the losses. Usually they elect a committee to manage the business. Examples of cooperatives are farming, production and retailing. Credit unions are a form of financial cooperative.

### SUMMARY QUESTIONS

1 What types of business are owned by shareholders?

2 List the other types of businesses, and the owners of each type.

### KEY POINTS

- There are five main types of private sector organisation.
- Sole traders and partnerships are easy to set up, but have limited capital and unlimited liability.
- Companies are more complex to set up but give access to more capital, and shareholders have the protection of limited liability.

# Section 2    Practice exam questions

1 Producing and selling lots of different products would be classified as:

  a  A technical economy of scale

  b  A risk-spreading economy of scale

  c  A diseconomy of scale

  d  A financial economy of scale

2 A market stall sells cookies at $1 each. The stall costs $20 to rent and each cookie costs $0.30 to produce. If the stallholder bakes and sells 100 cookies, what will the *average total cost* be?

  a  $0.50

  b  $0.30

  c  $0.20

  d  $1.00

3 Which of the following types of economic system is most widely found in Caribbean countries?

  a  Traditional economies

  b  Free market economies

  c  Planned economies

  d  Mixed economies

4 In a planned economy, who makes most of the decisions about what to produce, and about who will receive goods and services?

  a  Individual consumers

  b  Private companies

  c  Government officials

  d  Households

5 The optimum size of a business is the point at which:

  a  Profits are highest

  b  Average costs are lowest

  c  Fixed costs are lowest

  d  Variable costs are falling

6 Diseconomies of scale result when:

  a  A firm increases in size

  b  Short-term average costs start to rise

  c  Inefficiencies result from a firm's increasing size

  d  Variable costs of production start to fall

7 Which of the following forms of business organisation is most likely to benefit from limited liability?

  a  Partnerships

  b  Sole traders

  c  Public companies

  d  All of the above

8 The following table illustrates the costs of production of a business:

| Output per week | Variable cost | Total cost per week |
|---|---|---|
| 0 | 0 | 200 |
| 5 | 25 | 225 |
| 10 | 40 | 240 |
| 15 | 50 | 250 |
| 20 | 70 | 270 |

What is the fixed cost of producing 10 units per week?

  a  $40

  b  $200

  c  $240

  d  There are not enough data to answer the question

9 Which of the following describes a typical average variable cost curve?

  a  It is U-shaped

  b  It continually falls from left to right

  c  It increases throughout its length

  d  It is a straight line

**10** Average cost can be calculated in the following way:

a Total cost times output

b Total cost divided by output

c Output level minus total cost

d Total cost plus output

## SECTION 2: Structured questions

**1 a** Explain the difference between *goods* and *services*, giving examples of each. (*4 marks*)

b Show how the productivity of labour is measured. (*2 marks*)

c Outline two reasons why the production of goods in an economy might rise, while productivity in the economy falls at the same time. (*4 marks*)

d Explain how the division of labour can be used to increase productivity. (*5 marks*)

**2 a** Paul owns a small supermarket. He has invested in fixtures and fittings such as shelves and computerised check-out tills to make his store attractive and efficient. Identify two factors of production (not including labour) that Paul would use and describe the rewards to these factors. (*4 marks*)

b Explain how the average productivity of labour employed in the supermarket will change when the number of workers employed increases or decreases. (*6 marks*)

c Explain why some Caribbean economies have available to them a higher proportion of skilled workers than other Caribbean economies. (*5 marks*)

**3 a** Define *division of labour*. (*2 marks*)

b Describe two advantages of division of labour in a factory. (*4 marks*)

c Describe two disadvantages of division of labour in a factory. (*4 marks*)

d Explain how a capital-intensive industry would differ from a labour-intensive one. (*5 marks*)

**4 a** Define economies of scale. (*2 marks*)

b Describe three economies of scale that would benefit a large hotel chain. (*6 marks*)

c Illustrate the impact of economies of scale on the average cost curve of a business over time. Explain your diagram. (*6 marks*)

d Describe three ways in which a business may suffer from diseconomies of scale. (*6 marks*)

**5 a** Outline the main features of a *traditional economy*. (*3 marks*)

b Explain four main differences between a planned economy and a market economy. (*8 marks*)

c Outline three types of economic system in the Caribbean. State the benefits and drawbacks of adopting one of these systems. (*5 marks*)

d Give two benefits for a planned economy that liberalises to become more market focused. (*4 marks*)

## 3.1

# Markets and market forces

Markets such as this one in Kingston, Jamaica, bring together buyers and sellers. Through demand, buyers are able to show their preferences for goods that they want supplied

**EXAM TIP**

Make sure you can explain how the market helps to coordinate the decisions of demanders and suppliers.

### The market

The **market** brings together buyers and sellers. This might be in a traditional market, where buyers and sellers come together to trade for vegetables, meat, clothing and other items. The term also describes any other situation where buyers and sellers contact each other. They might do this over the telephone or on the internet.

The market brings together two sets of people: those who are willing and able to buy products (demanders), and those who are willing and able to supply products (suppliers) – see Figure 3.1.1.

| **Figure 3.1.1** | Participants in the market |

**CASE STUDY**    The fruit market at Georgetown, Guyana

Mango, star fruit and pawpaw are some of the types of fruit for sale at the market in Starboek, in Georgetown. Because fruit deteriorates quickly the suppliers want to sell all their stock on the day of the market. Buyers range from householders buying a few items to eat on the day, to commercial buyers looking to stock hotel and restaurant kitchens. The suppliers will look around to see what rival competitors are charging: they cannot pitch their price much above the daily market price or they will have unsold stocks at the end of the day. The demanders will want high-quality, fresh produce at the best prices. They will also look around to make sure that they are not paying more than the market price. The result of all this competition is that a market price is reached where suppliers offer very similar prices for their fruit (depending on its quality and freshness). The two forces of demand and supply thus interact to create a market price.

The market price for different types of fruit will vary from month to month depending on which fruits are in season. When mangos are plentiful, for example, there will be lots of sellers, leading to more competition and lower prices. When mangos are less plentiful there will be fewer sellers and demanders will be willing to pay higher prices.

## Demand and supply

Economists use **demand** to mean the quantity of a good or service that consumers will be prepared to buy at a particular price. For example, at a price of 10 cents per mango, demanders at the fruit market in Georgetown, Guyana are willing and able to buy 1200 mangos on 14 June 2011.

Economists use **supply** to mean the quantity of a good or service that suppliers will be prepared to supply at a particular price. For example, at a price of 10 cents per mango, suppliers at the fruit market in Georgetown, Guyana are willing and able to supply 1200 mangos on 14 June 2011.

## Benefits of the market

The principal benefits of the market are as follows:

• It brings together buyers and sellers.

• It helps to allocate resources to goods that are in demand. For example, if a farmer knows that there are good prices to be gained from growing carrots, he will plant more of them.

• Coordinating decision-making: the market system coordinates billions of decisions. Across the world, every second, billions of consumers are making purchasing decisions. They make their decisions known through the purchases that they make. Sellers also make their own decisions about what to produce and sell.

• Providing plenty of choice: in a market that is working well, customers have choices; there will be plenty of competing rivals providing goods.

• Keeping prices down: competition in the market helps to keep prices down. Rival businesses will seek to beat the competition by providing lower prices than those offered by rivals.

# Price, demand and supply

**EXAM TIP**

There are two laws of demand and two laws of supply that you should learn. These laws explain what is likely to happen to the price in the market when (a) demand changes (laws of demand) and (b) supply changes (laws of supply).

## The four laws of demand and supply

There are four basic laws that you should learn about the relationship between supply, demand and the market price. The market price is the price at which goods and services are exchanged as a result of the interaction of market forces.

The four laws are:

1 If demand increases and supply remains constant, the market price will increase and suppliers will be encouraged to increase the quantity supplied.

2 If demand decreases and supply remains constant, the market price will fall and suppliers will be likely to reduce the quantity supplied.

3 If supply increases and demand remains constant, the market price will fall.

4 If supply decreases and demand remains constant, the market price will rise.

| CASE STUDY | The supply and demand for dry coconut |
|---|---|

Table 3.2.1 illustrates the demand and supply of dry coconut in a Caribbean economy. It shows the quantity that suppliers (growers) are willing to supply to the market and the quantity that demanders (companies purchasing dry coconut) are willing and able to buy at different prices.

**Table 3.2.1**

| Price per tonne ($) | Demand for coconut (tonnes) | Supply of coconut (tonnes) |
|---|---|---|
| 500 | 900 | 300 |
| 750 | 800 | 400 |
| 1000 | 700 | 500 |
| 1250 | 600 | 600 |
| 1500 | 500 | 700 |
| 1750 | 400 | 800 |
| 2000 | 300 | 900 |

In the case study the equilibrium market price is $1250 per tonne of dry coconut. This is the price determined by market forces. Demanders are willing to buy 600 tonnes of coconut and suppliers are willing to supply this quantity.

## The two laws of demand

What would happen if the demand for dry coconut increased or decreased while the supply remained constant? These situations are illustrated in Table 3.2.2. You can see that at each price, 200 more tonnes are demanded when demand rises, and 200 fewer tonnes are demanded when demand falls.

**Table 3.2.2 Supply and demand of dried coconut**

| Price per tonne ($) | Original demand (tonnes) | Supply (tonnes) | Demand rises (tonnes) | Demand falls (tonnes) |
|---|---|---|---|---|
| 500 | 900 | 300 | 1100 | 700 |
| 750 | 800 | 400 | 1000 | 600 |
| 1000 | 700 | 500 | 900 | 500 |
| 1250 | 600 | 600 | 800 | 400 |
| 1500 | 500 | 700 | 700 | 300 |
| 1750 | 400 | 800 | 600 | 200 |
| 2000 | 300 | 900 | 500 | 100 |

Table 3.2.2 illustrates the two laws of demand. You should be able to see that when demand rises (the fourth column), demand and supply match at a price of $1500 per tonne: suppliers are willing to supply 700 tonnes and demanders are willing to buy 700 tonnes. When demand falls (the fifth column), demand and supply match at a price of $1000 per tonne. Suppliers are now willing to supply 500 tonnes and demanders are willing to buy 500 tonnes.

**EXAM TIP**

Make sure you learn the laws of demand and can outline the likely effect of a change in demand while supply remains constant. An increase in demand means that more will be demanded at each possible price, leading to an increase in the market price. A decrease in demand means that less will be demanded at each possible price, leading to a fall in market price.

EXAM TIP

The laws of supply outline the likely effects of a change in supply while demand remains constant. When supply increases, the market price will fall. When supply decreases the market price will rise.

## The two laws of supply

What will happen if the supply of dried coconut increases or decreases while the demand remains constant? These situations are illustrated in Table 3.2.3.

Table 3.2.3 The two laws of supply

| Price per tonne ($) | Demand (tonnes) | Original supply (tonnes) | Supply rises (tonnes) | Supply falls (tonnes) |
|---|---|---|---|---|
| 500 | 900 | 300 | 500 | 100 |
| 750 | 800 | 400 | 600 | 200 |
| 1000 | 700 | 500 | 700 | 300 |
| 1250 | 600 | 600 | 800 | 400 |
| 1500 | 500 | 700 | 900 | 500 |
| 1750 | 400 | 800 | 1000 | 600 |
| 2000 | 300 | 900 | 1100 | 700 |

Demand is initially equal to supply at a market price of $1250 per tonne, that is where demand is 600 tonnes and supply is 600 tonnes. Columns 4 and 5 of Table 3.2.3 illustrate a rise in supply (column 4) and a fall in supply (column 5).

When supply rises by 200 tonnes at each price (column 4), demand and supply will be in equilibrium (equal to each other) at a price of $1000. At $1000 demand will be 700 tonnes and supply will be 700 tonnes.

In contrast, when supply falls at each price by 200 tonnes (column 5), demand and supply will be in equilibrium at a price of $1500. At $1500, demand will be 500 tonnes and supply will be 500 tonnes. The new price is higher than the original price.

Demand and supply for most products changes frequently. When economists talk about market forces they are referring to changes in demand and supply. The relative strength of demand and supply determines the market prices of goods. Market prices act as signals to producers about the strength of demand for the products they supply. Rising prices act as an incentive for producers to produce more of certain types of goods. In contrast, falling prices will encourage consumers to buy more of goods as they become relatively cheaper. Gaining a clear understanding of the four laws of demand and supply will enable you to have a good grasp of how the market works.

### DID YOU KNOW?

The prices of food, oil and water are increasing at a global level because demand for them is increasing faster than supply.

SUMMARY QUESTIONS

1 What will happen to market price if:

a demand stays the same and supply increases

b supply decreases and demand stays the same

c demand increases and supply stays the same?

2 Explain which of the laws of demand and supply is involved in the following situations, and what the likely impact on price would be in each case:

a The demand for fresh tomatoes increases in Jamaica while the supply remains constant.

b The supply of butter fish in the Caribbean falls while demand reamins constant.

c The number of new hotels opening up in Barbados increases while the number of people seeking hotel accommodation remains the same.

d There is a fall in demand for suntan lotion resulting from poor weather, while the supply of suntan lotion remains the same.

e There is an increase in the number of private buses operating on bus routes in Barbados, while the number of passengers remains the same.

f There is an increase in the demand for Jamaican coffee while the supply remains the same.

g As a result of a hurricane there is a fall in food supplies while demand remains the same.

# Demand and supply curves

**Table 3.3.1 Demand for dried coconut at different prices**

| Price per tonne ($) | Quantity demanded (tonnes) |
|---|---|
| 500 | 900 |
| 750 | 800 |
| 1000 | 700 |
| 1250 | 600 |
| 1500 | 500 |
| 1750 | 400 |
| 2000 | 300 |

## Demand curves

A demand curve is used by economists to illustrate the relationship between price and quantity demanded. It shows demand, and changes in quantity demanded. It is useful for business organisations trying to predict the effect of different prices on demand for their products. It helps them to decide how many to make in order to meet quantity demanded.

Common sense and personal experience explain the shape of the demand curve. The curve slopes down from left to right because more people can afford to buy goods at lower rather than at higher prices. Existing purchasers of a good will be tempted to buy more of a good at a lower price because they have to give up less of their income to make the purchase. Table 3.3.1 and Figure 3.3.1 show the quantity demanded for dried coconut at different prices per tonne.

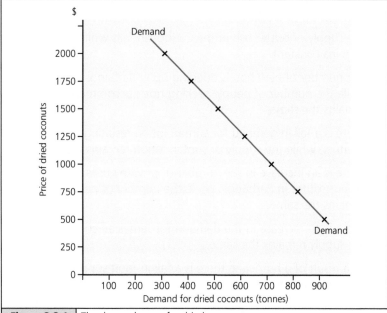

**Figure 3.3.1** | The demand curve for dried coconut

The demand curve is constructed by showing prices on the vertical axis and quantities demanded along the horizontal axis. You can see that:

• higher prices lead to lower quantities being bought

• lower prices lead to higher quantities being bought.

## Supply curves

The supply of a product is the quantity that a supplier is willing to provide at different prices. Typically, suppliers will supply more at higher prices than at lower prices. Higher prices enable producers to cover costs and increase their profits.

Table 3.3.2 shows the supply curve for dried coconut at different prices.

The supply curve is constructed by showing quantity supplied along the horizontal axis and price along the vertical axis. You can see that:

- higher prices lead to greater quantities being supplied
- lower prices lead to smaller quantities being supplied.

Figure 3.3.2 shows the supply curve.

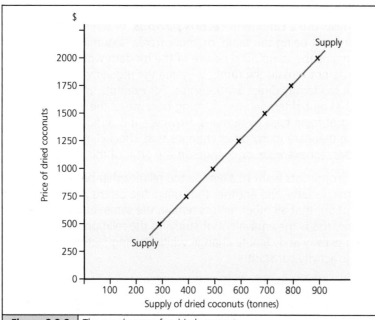

**Table 3.3.2 Supply of dried coconut at different prices**

| Price per tonne ($) | Quantity supplied (tonnes) |
| --- | --- |
| 500 | 300 |
| 750 | 400 |
| 1000 | 500 |
| 1250 | 600 |
| 1500 | 700 |
| 1750 | 800 |
| 2000 | 900 |

**Figure 3.3.2** The supply curve for dried coconut

## Combining the demand and supply curves

Demand and supply curves for a product can be plotted onto a single diagram. Where the demand and supply curves intersect is the **equilibrium price**. Figure 3.3.3 shows the demand and supply curve for dried coconut – the economist's way of representing the market for this product. Note that the equilibrium price is at $1250.

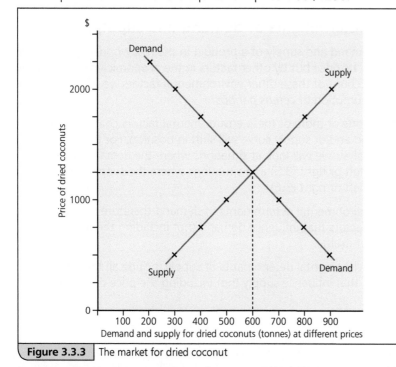

**Figure 3.3.3** The market for dried coconut

# Demand and supply conditions

Candidates should be able to:

• explain the concept of *ceteris paribus*

• explain the determinants of demand and supply.

---

*Ceteris paribus* =
assuming everything else remains the same

---

## *Ceteris paribus*

Economists use a Latin term **ceteris paribus**, which means literally 'with the rest being the same' or, more freely, 'assuming everything else remains the same'. The nature of the modern world is that many things do not remain the same: they change regularly. This makes it difficult to identify direct relationships. For example, many scientists think that global temperature is rising because of the increased burning of fossil fuels by humans. However, it is difficult to prove this because there are many other changes that affect climate – volcanic eruptions, for example, or changes in the orbit of the Earth.

When economists want to examine the relationship between one economic variable and another they make the *ceteris paribus* assumption, that all other factors remain the same. In our climate example, this is the equivalent of studying the relationship between human activity and climate change while holding factors such as volcanic activity constant.

For example, economists look at the relationship between:

• the demand for a product and its price *ceteris paribus*

• the supply of a product and its price *ceteris paribus*.

This enables us to draw a demand curve showing the relationship between price and quantity demanded *ceteris paribus*. We can also draw a supply curve showing the relationship between price and quantity supplied *ceteris paribus*.

When we assume *ceteris paribus,* the only factor affecting the quantity demanded or supplied of a product is its price.

## The determinants of demand and supply

The demand and supply of a product in the real world is affected not only by its price but by other factors in the economic environment. To take account of these other environmental factors we need to remove the assumption of *ceteris paribus*.

When one or more of these environmental factors changes, the demand and/or supply curve will shift in position. For the purpose of our analysis we will look at situations where the demand curve shifts to the left or right (3.5) and situations where the supply curve shifts to the left or right (3.6).

The environmental determinants of demand therefore include all the other factors that influence demand (not including the price of the product itself).

The environmental determinants of supply include all the other factors that influence supply (not including the price of the product itself).

A movement down a demand curve is called an *extension in demand*. A movement up a demand curve is called a *contraction in demand*. A movement down a supply curve is called a *contraction in supply*. A movement up a supply curve is called an *extension in supply*.

## Movements along a curve

When the only factor influencing demand or supply is the price of the product itself, this will lead to a movement up or down the demand or supply curve.

When factors other than the price of the product change, this is likely to lead to a shift in the demand or supply curve.

Figure 3.4.1 shows a movement down a demand curve resulting from the fall in price of a product.

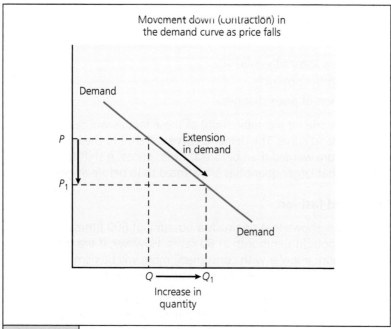

**Figure 3.4.1** | Movements along a demand curve

**Table 3.4.1 Extension and contraction in demand and supply**

| What happens | Term used |
| --- | --- |
| Demand increases as a result of a fall in price (*ceteris paribus*) | Extension in demand |
| Demand falls as a result of a fall in price (*ceteris paribus*) | Contraction in demand |
| Supply increases as a result of a rise in price (*ceteris paribus*) | Extension in supply |
| Supply falls as a result of a fall in price (*ceteris paribus*) | Contraction in supply |

**EXAM TIP**

Make sure that you are clear in your own mind about the difference between movements (contractions and extensions) in demand and supply, and shifts to the whole demand or supply curve.

**SUMMARY QUESTIONS**

1 Why is important to make the *ceteris paribus* assumption when drawing demand and supply curves?

2 Explain three determinants of demand and three determinants of supply.

**KEY POINTS**

- *Ceteris paribus* means all other things remaining the same.
- The *ceteris paribus* assumption is used when examining the relationship between two variables, for example demand and income, while leaving unchanged anything else that would be likely to affect demand.

# Changes in the conditions of demand

When fitness drinks become more popular the demand for them shifts to the right

## Changes in the conditions of demand

In addition to price, there are a number of factors that influence the demand for a product. If one of these factors alters, the conditions of demand are said to have changed. These factors include:

• tastes or fashion
• income
• number of buyers/population
• price of other products
• expectation of price changes.

Changes in one (or a combination) of these factors will cause a shift in the demand curve. The demand curve will shift to the left if smaller quantities are wanted than before at given prices. A shift to the right indicates that larger quantities are wanted than before at given prices.

### Tastes and fashion

Figure 3.5.1 shows that originally a quantity of 600 fitness drinks would be bought per month at 80 cents. However, if the drinks become more popular with consumers, more will be demanded at all prices, so that, for example, at 80 cents perhaps 800 will be bought.

Alternatively if the drinks become less popular, fewer will be bought at all prices so that at 80 cents 400 drinks will now be demanded.

### Income

It is obviously easier to buy goods if you have money to spend. The amount of income people have to spend on goods – that is, after essentials such as food have been bought – is known as their **disposable income**. Average incomes tend to rise over time, which

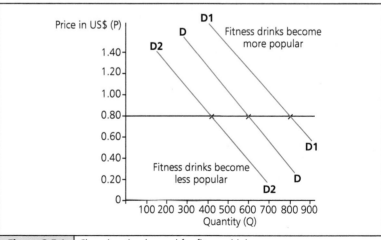

| **Figure 3.5.1** | Changing the demand for fitness drinks |

leads to a general increase in demand for most goods, noticeably expensive branded goods. An increase in incomes leads to a shift to the right in the demand curve.

However, some products may become less popular as income rises: as spending power increases they may be regarded as inferior. An example is a bicycle being replaced by a motor scooter or a car. In the case of inferior goods, when incomes rise, demand shifts to the left. This **income elasticity of demand** is explained in 3.10. Most goods have a positive **income elasticity**. As income rises, more of the good is purchased. In contrast, inferior goods have negative income elasticity, showing that as incomes rise people buy fewer of these goods.

## Number of buyers and population

The size of the population can affect demand. For example, in the holiday season thousands of tourists come to the Caribbean islands, increasing the demand for food and many other items, thus pushing up prices.

## Price of other products

The demand for products that have close substitutes will often be strongly influenced by the price of the substitutes. This would be the case, for example, with different brands of tinned fruit or different brands of petrol: there are many similar brand names from which consumers can choose.

The demand curve for a product is likely to shift to the right if a substitute product rises in price. The demand curve for a product is likely to shift to the left if a substitute product falls in price.

Some products are used together (**complementary goods**), and the demand for one is linked to the price of another. An example might be restaurant meals and drinks sold in restaurants: if the price of a restaurant meal falls, this is likely to lead to an increase in demand for drinks.

## Expectation of price changes

Expectation that prices will change in the future will also affect the demand for a product. For example, if people think that prices are due to rise shortly, they will want to hoard goods to protect themselves against the rise.

**EXAM TIP**

You need to show that you understand that a shift of a demand curve takes place when something happens in a market other than a change in the price of a product.

**DID YOU KNOW?**

Ferry travel can become an inferior good, if inter-island travellers choose to travel by air as their incomes rise. This will depend, however, on the reliability of the air travel.

**KEY POINTS**

- Shifts in demand result from changes in factors other than price.
- Changes in taste, income, population and the price of other goods all lead to a shift in the demand curve.

**SUMMARY QUESTIONS**

Refer to Figure 3.5.2.

1 Which of the following changes would cause a shift to $D_1 D_1$?
   a a health warning about the bad effects of chewing spearmint-flavoured gum
   b a fall in the price of other flavours of gum
   c an advertising campaign for spearmint gum

2 Which of the above would cause a shift to $D_2 D_2$ for spearmint chewing gum?

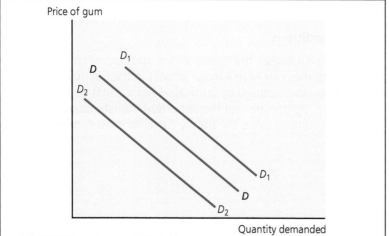

**Figure 3.5.2** | Demand for spearmint gum

# Changes in the conditions of supply

One of the effects of a hurricane will be a shift to the left in the supply curve for many goods

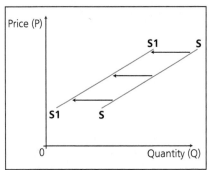

| Figure 3.6.1 | The effect of a shift in the supply curve |

## Shifts in the supply curve

The cost of producing an item is determined by the price of the various inputs, including the raw materials and machinery used to make it. Rises in the prices of some resource inputs will increase production costs, which in turn results in a reduction in supply at each price rise (Figure 3.6.1). The supply curve shifts to the left when, at any given price, fewer items are produced and offered for sale.

## Causes of changes in supply conditions

There are several factors that can cause changes in supply:

• rising or falling production costs
• changes in technology
• changes in physical conditions
• changes in taxation and subsidies
• changes in joint supply conditions
• changes in the number of producers.

### Rising or falling production costs

A rise in production costs pushes the supply curve to the left (it will cost more to produce each level of output), and a fall in production costs pushes the supply curve to the right.

Rising resource prices lead to rising production costs. War and conflict can restrict the supply of important resources such as oil and can lead to rapid increases in production costs. Production costs fall when the price of resources falls. So when the price of oil falls, energy costs for all industries are reduced.

### Changes in technology

The development of new technology in the form of computer-based processing systems and computer-controlled machinery has reduced production costs in many industries, pushing the supply curve to the right.

### Physical conditions

Changes in the weather, the quality of soil and natural disasters such as hurricanes can have a major impact in the Caribbean. The physical devastation caused by hurricanes has a negative effect on infrastructure, agriculture and the important tourist industry. The effect of hurricanes pushes the supply curve for most products to the left.

## Taxation and subsidies

Rises in taxation and subsidies pull in opposite directions on the supply curve. A production tax of 10 cents per unit on a good would increase the cost of its production by 10 cents per unit. In contrast, a subsidy would reduce the costs of production. Supply therefore shifts to the left as a result of rising taxes on a product, and to the right as a result of a subsidy (Figure 3.6.2).

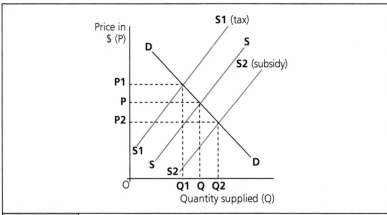

| Figure 3.6.2 | The impact of taxes and subsidies on the supply of a product |

## Joint supply

Some production processes create more than one product (joint supply). In the Caribbean, oil and natural gas are in many instances produced as part of the same process. Increases in oil supply therefore drive down the prices of these by-products as more of them are supplied to market.

## Number of producers

An increase in the number of producers will usually increase the supply of a product. Where suppliers leave the market this can reduce the supply.

## Effects of changes in supply on the market

An increase in supply results in a fall in the price of a product. This leads to a movement along the demand curve (more is bought in response to the lower price).

A decrease in supply results in a rise in the price of a product. This leads to a movement along the demand curve (less is bought in response to the higher price).

# 3.7

# Equilibrium price

**LEARNING OUTCOMES**

Candidates should be able to:

- explain the concept of market equilibrium
- illustrate changes in the market equilibrium.

The price that the coconut seller charges is determined by demand and supply. The higher the price, the more the supplier will bring to market. The lower the price, the more consumers will want to buy

**EXAM TIP**

The equilibrium position in a market will be where demand and supply intersect. When you draw this in a diagram you will need to make sure that you clearly show the equilibrium price on the vertical axis and the equilibrium quantity on the horizontal.

## Equilibrium price

Equilibrium means a state of balance. **Equilibrium price** occurs when there is a balance between demand and supply: the quantity demanded by consumers is equal to the amount that suppliers are willing to provide. For example, Ramesh and his family collect fresh coconuts in a plantation that they own. They sell them at a local holiday beach. The higher the price they can get, the more they will supply. The lower the price that Ramesh charges, the more customers will buy his coconuts (they can always buy from rival sellers).

The table of demand and supply schedules shows the weekly demand and supply for Ramesh's coconuts:

| Price of Ramesh's coconuts ($) | Supply per week | Demand per week |
|---|---|---|
| 2.50 | 500 | 200 |
| 2.00 | 400 | 400 |
| 1.50 | 300 | 600 |
| 1.00 | 200 | 800 |

These demand and supply curves can be illustrated on a single drawing, as in Figure 3.7.1.

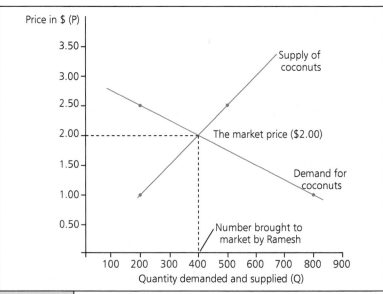

| **Figure 3.7.1** | How the price of Ramesh's coconuts is determined |

You can now see that, at a price of $2.00 per coconut, 400 would be bought each week. At this price Ramesh's customers would be happy to buy all 400 and Ramesh would be happy to supply this quantity.

This is the equilibrium price, as both seller and buyer are happy with the price.

You can see why this point is an equilibrium one by considering non-equilibrium points. For example, at $2.50 Ramesh would be prepared to supply 500 coconuts, but buyers would only be prepared to purchase 200 (leaving 300 unsold). Alternatively, if we examine a price below the market one ($1.00), customers would be willing to buy 800 coconuts, but Ramesh would be prepared to bring 200 to sell. Customers would soon bid the price back up to the equilibrium price.

The market price is often referred to as the **market clearing price**, because demand matches the quantity supplied. Therefore the market would be 'cleared', with no coconuts remaining and no dissatisfied customers.

---

**CASE STUDY** | The market for cement in Trinidad

Trinidad is a major supplier of cement to the Caribbean region, producing over a million tonnes each year. In recent years there have been some major changes. These include: an increase in demand in the Caribbean for cement for construction, rising costs of producing cement resulting from the rise in the cost of natural gas, disruption to production from hurricanes, and increases in subsidies by the government to Trinidad cement manufacturers to help them compete with cheap imported cement from China. In 2011 the market price was about $850 per tonne.

**Questions**

1 For each of the changes mentioned in this case study, show what the impact would be on the market for cement, starting from a position of a market price of $850 per tonne and a supply of 1 million tonnes.

2 Identify whether supply or demand curves would shift, whether they would shift to the left or right, and what the impact would be on prices.

---

## The effect of changes in demand and supply on the market

The effect is summarised in Table 3.7.1.

**Table 3.7.1 Effect of demand and supply changes**

| | Effect on equilibrium market price | Effect on equilibrium market quantity |
|---|---|---|
| Demand shifts to the right | Increases | Increases |
| Demand shifts to the left | Falls | Falls |
| Supply shifts to the right | Falls | Increases |
| Supply shifts to the left | Increases | Falls |

**SUMMARY QUESTIONS**

1 Draw a diagram to show how the market equilibrium would change for flights to Barbados resulting from a rise in demand from US tourists, assuming *ceteris paribus*.

2 Draw a diagram to show how the market equilibrium would change for bauxite from Jamaica, assuming that supplies run short in competitor countries *ceteris paribus*.

## EXAM TIP

It is important to understand the difference between a change in demand and a change in the quantity demanded. A change in demand involves a shift in the demand curve. A change in the quantity demanded results from a change in the price of that good. The same distinction can be applied to a change in supply and a change in the quantity supplied.

Changes in market equilibrium result from changes in the market environment – that is, shifts in the demand and supply curves.

Figure 3.8.1 illustrates the effect of an increase in demand for an expensive brand of trainers. This might be triggered by the rising popularity of the brand, an increase in consumer incomes, an increase in the population of consumers (mainly young people) or a fall in the price of a good that complements the sneakers, for example designer clothes or tracksuits. The diagram illustrates the impact of the change. Demand shifts from DD to $D_1D_1$ leading to an increase in price from P to $P_1$ and an increase in the quantity traded on the market from Q to $Q_1$.

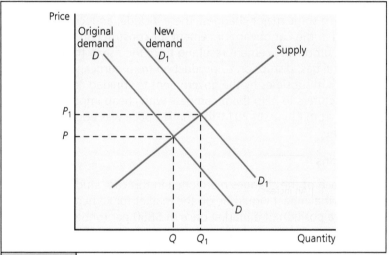

**Figure 3.8.1** | An increase in demand for sneakers

Figure 3.8.2 illustrates the effect of a fall in demand for tourist holidays to a popular destination. This might be a result of adverse weather conditions in the region, political unrest or steep price rises in the visitors' home market. You can see that the market price charged by tour operators would fall from P to $P_1$, and the quantity of holidays traded in the market would fall from Q to $Q_1$.

Figure 3.8.3 shows the impact of a shift in the supply of fish to a fish market in Grenada. There are a number of reasons why the supply might increase, including an increase in the number of fishermen, an increase in fish stocks in the sea, the use of better techniques for catching fish (including better equipment), a fall in fishing costs (for example cheaper fuel) or a subsidy paid by the government to encourage fishing.

You can see that the impact of the shift in the supply to the right is to increase the supply to the market and to lower the market price.

Changes in demand for items like trainers can bring about changes in market equilibrium

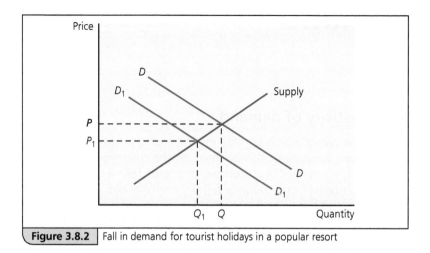

**Figure 3.8.2** | Fall in demand for tourist holidays in a popular resort

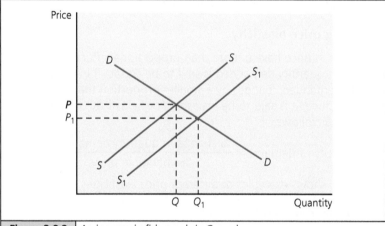

**Figure 3.8.3** | An increase in fish supply in Grenada

Figure 3.8.4, the final illustration in this sequence, shows the impact of a reduction in sugar cane production in the Caribbean on the regional sugar market. What factors can you think of that would cause the supply curve to shift to the left?

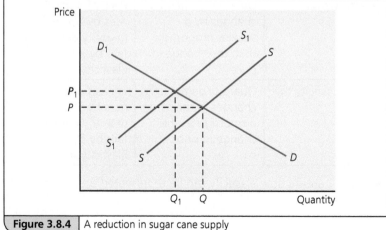

**Figure 3.8.4** | A reduction in sugar cane supply

# Price elasticity of demand

**LEARNING OUTCOMES**

Candidates should be able to:

- explain the concept of price elasticity of demand
- illustrate price elasticity of demand using simple calculations.

As incomes rise people start to buy more expensive products

**DID YOU KNOW?**

Price elasticity of demand is always a minus figure. This is because an increase in price (+) leads to a fall in quantity demanded (−). A fall in price (−) leads to a rise in quantity demanded (+). Another way of putting this is that there is an inverse relationship between price and quantity demanded.

**DID YOU KNOW?**

If the demand for a good is inelastic, an increase in its price will lead to an increase in revenue to the seller. In contrast, where demand is elastic, an increase in a good's price will lead to a fall in revenue to the seller.

## Price elasticity of demand

A restaurant owner who is considering increasing prices will first want to know what effect this will have on the customers. Will there be no effect, a small fall in customers, or a large fall? If the number of customers remains the same or falls by a smaller percentage than the price change, the business will make more revenue. The calculation used to estimate this effect is **price elasticity of demand**, which measures how quantity demanded for a product responds to a change in its price. Anyone wishing to raise or lower prices should first estimate the **price elasticity**.

### Measuring price elasticity

Where falls in price have a more than proportional effect on quantity demanded, quantity demanded is said to be *elastic*. If instead quantity demanded changes by a smaller proportion than the change in price, it is said to be *inelastic*. Price elasticity of demand is calculated as follows:

$$\text{Price elasticity of demand} = \frac{\text{\% change in quantity demanded}}{\text{\% change in price}}$$

Table 3.9.1 shows examples of different price elasticities.

**Table 3.9.1 Relative elasticities**

| Relative elasticity | Description | Example |
|---|---|---|
| Elastic demand | Quantity demanded changes by a larger proportion than the change in price | Price of a good rises by 5% while quantity demanded falls by 10% Elasticity = −2 |
| Inelastic demand | Quantity demanded changes by a smaller proportion than the change in price | Price of a good rises by 5% while quantity demanded falls by 2.5% Elasticity = −½ |
| Unitary elasticity of demand | Quantity demanded changes in the same proportion as the change in price | Price of a good rises by 5% while quantity demanded falls by 5% Elasticity = −1 |

Figure 3.9.1 shows how elasticity can be represented on a chart.

| Inelastic demand | | | | Unitary | | | Elastic demand | |
|---|---|---|---|---|---|---|---|---|
| $-\frac{1}{20}$ | $-\frac{1}{10}$ | $-\frac{1}{5}$ | $-\frac{1}{2}$ | $-1$ | $-2$ | $-5$ | $-10$ | $-20$ |

**Figure 3.9.1** | Elasticity

## How to make simple calculations

**1** Calculate the percentage change in quantity demanded. This is the change in quantity demanded as a percentage of the quantity originally demanded (before the price change).

**2** Calculate the percentage change in price. This is the change in price as a percentage of the original price (before the price change).

**3** Divide the percentage change in quantity demanded by the percentage change in price. Remember to include the minus sign.

**4** If the figure is greater than −1, demand is relatively elastic. If it is less than −1, demand is relatively inelastic.

## Illustrating elastic demand

**Example:** Elastic demand can be illustrated by a relatively flat demand curve showing that quantity demanded changes by a greater proportion than the change in price.

A ferry company reduces fares from $1 to 90 cents. Daily demand for tickets rises from 10 000 to 12 000 (Figure 3.9.2). Price elasticity is therefore −2 (elastic demand):

$$\frac{20\%}{-10\%} = -2$$

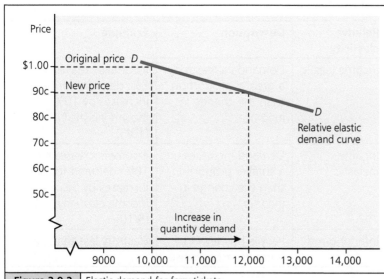

**Figure 3.9.2** | Elastic demand for ferry tickets

# Income elasticity and cross elasticity

The demand for red snapper is affected by the price of sardines (cross elasticity)

## DID YOU KNOW?

The relationship between income and demand is in most cases a direct one rather than an inverse one. As incomes rise so too does the demand for most goods and services.

## Income elasticity of demand

In most countries average incomes increase over time. As this happens, people alter their consumption pattern, for example they are likely to purchase more luxury goods. It is useful therefore for sellers to know how the demand for the goods they are selling is likely to alter as incomes rise. Income elasticity of demand is measured in the following way:

$$\text{Income elasticity} = \frac{\text{Percentage change in demand}}{\text{Percentage change in income}}$$

For normal goods – that is, goods that people are more likely to buy when their incomes rise – income elasticity will be above zero.

Some goods have an income elasticity greater than 1, showing that the percentage change in demand is greater than the percentage change in income. This situation is described as *income elastic*.

Other goods may have an income elasticity of less than 1, showing that the percentage change in demand is less than the percentage change in income. This situation is described as *income inelastic*. Goods affected are inferior goods – that is, those that people are less likely to buy when their incomes rise.

Table 3.10.1 shows examples of the effect of some different income elasticities.

**Table 3.10.1**

| Relative elasticity | Description | Example |
|---|---|---|
| Income elastic | Demand increases by a greater proportion than the change in income | Income increases by 5%: demand for good increases by 10% Income elasticity = 2 (10/5) |
| Income inelastic | Demand increases by a smaller proportion than the change in income | Income increases by 10%: demand for good increases by 5% Income elasticity = ½ (5/10) |
| Inferior good | People buy fewer of them as incomes rise | Elasticity less than zero |

## Cross-price elasticity of demand

**Cross-price elasticity** is a measure of the extent to which a change in the price of one good affects the demand for another good, whether it is a substitute good or a complementary good. Consider the rival demand for different types of fish, for example red snapper and sardines. An increase in the price of red snapper is likely to lead to a rise in demand for sardines, which are now cheaper by comparison.

Cross-price elasticity of demand is measured in the following way:

$$\text{Cross-price elasticity of demand} = \frac{\text{Percentage change in demand for product X}}{\text{Percentage change in price of product Y}}$$

If red snapper (product X) and sardines (product Y) are rivals, then as the price of sardines increases, the demand for red snapper will also increase.

The cross elasticity of demand between red snapper and sardines will lie somewhere between zero and plus infinity.

The cross elasticity of demand between red snapper and a complementary good will lie somewhere between zero and minus infinity. This is because there is an inverse relationship between demand and price for complementary goods.

## KEY POINTS

- Income elasticity of demand measures the responsiveness of demand of a good to a change in incomes.
- Cross elasticity of demand measures the responsiveness of the demand of a good to a change in the price of another good.

## SUMMARY QUESTION

What is the difference between:

a  price elasticity and cross elasticity

b  price elasticity and income elasticity?

# Price elasticity of supply

For goods that cannot be stored for long, such as this fresh produce in a market in Trinidad, price elasticity of supply is reduced

## Changes in supply

When the price of a good rises or falls, this leads to an **extension in supply** – that is, a movement up or down the supply curve. The extent to which quantity supplied responds to a change in price is determined by how elastic supply is.

### Price elasticity of supply

**Price elasticity of supply** is the extent to which quantity supplied alters in response to a change in price. It is measured by the formula:

$$\text{Price elasticity of supply} = \frac{\% \text{ change in quantity supplied}}{\% \text{ change in price}}$$

In the case of supply there is a positive relationship between the two variables. As a result price elasticity of supply will typically be represented by a + sign.

Elastic supply occurs when the percentage change in quantity supplied is greater than the percentage change in price, for example if supply increased by 10 per cent as a result of a 5 per cent increase in price.

### Factors influencing price elasticity of supply

The main factor influencing price elasticity of supply is time. At a particular moment in time it may be impossible to increase supply, for example reprinting a popular book, however much price increases. Supply in this instance is perfectly inelastic. In the short term it may be possible to increase supply using existing equipment and machinery. In the longer term it may be possible to increase supply further by acquiring more machinery and equipment. The longer the period of time, the more elastic supply is in response to a price change (Figure 3.11.1).

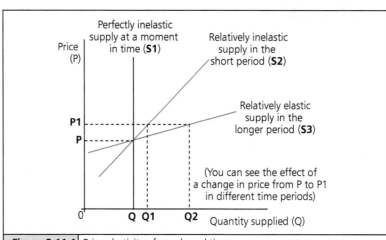

**Figure 3.11.1** Price elasticity of supply and time

In Figure 3.11.1, S1 shows **perfectly inelastic supply** at a moment in time, S2 shows relatively inelastic supply in the short period, and S3 represents relatively elastic supply in the longer period.

Other factors affecting price elasticity of supply are:

• The ease with which a product can be stored. If stores of a product can be kept easily, supply will be more elastic. Coffee can be stored in jars (making supply elastic), but fresh strawberries go off very quickly (making supply more inelastic).

• The cost of increasing supply. The less costly it is to increase supply, the more elastic supply will be.

## Making simple calculations

**Example 1:** A rise in the price of rice in a country from $1 per bag to $1.20 per bag leads to an increase in quantity supplied by farmers from 1000 bags per month to 1300 bags per month.

$$\text{Price elasticity of supply} = \frac{30 \text{ per cent}}{20 \text{ per cent}}$$

$$= 1.5 \text{ (relatively elastic supply)}$$

**Example 2:** There is a shortage of flour in a country. A rise in the price of bread from 50 cents to 60 cents a loaf leads to an increase in quantity supplied by bakers from 1000 loaves per month to 1100 loaves per month.

$$\text{Price elasticity of supply} = \frac{10 \text{ per cent}}{20 \text{ per cent}}$$

$$= 0.5 \text{ (relatively inelastic supply)}$$

### KEY POINTS

1 Price elasticity of supply measures the responsiveness of supply to changes in price.

2 Price elasticity of supply is a positive number.

3 Price elasticity of supply is calculated by dividing the percentage change in quantity supplied by the percentage change in price.

### SUMMARY QUESTION

Increasing demand for melons in a city pushed up the price per melon from 20 cents to 25 cents. This led to an increase in quantity supplied of melons per day from 2000 to 2500.

Calculate the price elasticity of supply.

### DID YOU KNOW?

We use the term *price elasticity of supply* because quantities supplied are responding to changes in the price of a good. The raised price gives an incentive to, or encourages, producers to supply more.

### EXAM TIP

Remember that when producers are not manufacturing at full capacity they could always produce a little more if the price increased. So when businesses have unused capacity, supply tends to be more elastic than if they are producing at full capacity. In a period of recession supply can be quite elastic, in that producers have the ability to supply more.

### EXAM TIP

Remember that the factors that affect demand and supply are different from those that affect a change in demand and supply.

# Market structures

The price of snow cones is low and competitive because there are many sellers

## What is market structure?

Market structure means the characteristics under which a market operates. It consists of four main elements:

- how easy it is for new firms to enter the market or for existing firms to leave
- the number of buyers and sellers
- the types of goods and services sold in the market
- how price is determined in the market.

### Extreme market structures

It is possible to identify two extreme market structures. At one extreme is a situation where the market is controlled by one supplier. This is referred to as a **monopoly**. For example, there is only one television station in Barbados: it therefore has no competing station. Competition is also limited in the oil industry in Trinidad, where companies have to have a licence from the government to drill for oil. At the other extreme there are competitive markets in which many sellers provide almost identical products, for example bag juice in Jamaica, or snow cones in Barbados.

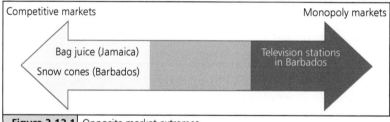

Competitive markets                                                Monopoly markets

Bag juice (Jamaica)
Snow cones (Barbados)                          Television stations in Barbados

| **Figure 3.12.1** | Opposite market extremes |

Table 3.12.1 summarises the four main types of market structure. These are explained in greater detail in 3.13 and 3.14.

In the past many Caribbean countries' bus routes were run by a single company – the state-run bus company. Today there is often fierce competition between rival bus companies offering different services, for example reggae bus companies playing reggae music along the way.

| CASE STUDY | Changing market structures in Antigua |

In 2010 in Antigua, there was much controversy about the arrival of the dollar bus to transport Antigua State College students. Until 2010 one bus driver dominated the route transporting Antigua State College students to St John's. The bus driver was used to charging $2.25 and was making good revenues and profits from the business.

However, another driver was not happy about the route being dominated by one company and set out to win a share of that market. He created the one-dollar bus route, charging just one dollar. Soon his bus was full as students queued to travel on his bus.

## Questions

1 What type of market structure did this bus route have when there was only one bus company serving it? Why was it possible to charge $2.25?

2 How would the entry of the one-dollar bus have changed the market structure on this particular route? What would you expect to be the impact on prices in the market?

Table 3.12.1 Types of market structure

| Market structure | Number of buyers and sellers | Types of goods | Freedom of entry | Price controls |
|---|---|---|---|---|
| Perfect competition | Many buyers and sellers | Goods all the same | Perfectly free entry | Firms are price takers |
| Monopolistic competition | Large numbers of buyers and several sellers | Goods are similar but differentiated | Free entry or easy access | Firms are price setters |
| Oligopoly | Large numbers of buyers, only a few sellers | Goods can be differentiated or homogeneous | Restrictions to entry | Firms are price setters |
| Monopoly | Many buyers, one seller | Only one producer | Very difficult for new firms to enter | Firms are price setters |

## Features of market structures

1 The number of buyers and sellers: most consumer markets have many buyers. In some markets for producer goods, for example machinery, there may be a smaller number of buyers. The number of sellers varies from just one in a pure monopoly situation to an infinite number in a perfectly competitive market.

2 Types of goods: some goods are identical (or almost identical) in nature, for example bags of white sugar. Other goods are highly differentiated, for example works of art painted by skilled, celebrated artists. The more sellers there are, the higher the level of competition.

3 Freedom of entry and exit: some markets are difficult to enter. For example, many professions, such as medicine, involve high levels of skill so there are relatively few practitioners. Other markets are easy to enter, for example to set up a business selling bag juice. The greater the ease of entry, the more intense the competition.

4 Controls on price: in most markets firms compete with each other through the prices they charge. However, in monopoly markets the monopolist is able to set prices. In some instances the government also sets price controls in the form of maximum prices that sellers can charge.

### KEY POINTS

- The number of buyers and sellers is a key determinant of how competitive a market is.
- The ease of entry to a market also affects the level of competition.
- In competitive markets firms take the price from the market. Monopoly businesses can set their own price.

### SUMMARY QUESTIONS

1 What is a market structure?

2 What markets can you think of where there are only one or two suppliers?

3 What markets can you think of where there are many suppliers?

# Perfect competition and monopoly

Candidates should be able to:

- identify and describe perfect competition
- identify and describe monopoly.

Some grades of grain are almost identical. The produce therefore creates a competitive market for grain – particularly if there are many producers

**DID YOU KNOW?**

**Normal profit** refers to the profit that a business needs to make to stay in a market. The normal profit that an entrepreneur will need to make is equivalent to what they could make from using their capital and talent in its next best use – that is, the opportunity cost of remaining in an industry. **Abnormal profit** refers to any profit made in excess of normal profit.

## Perfect competition

As a way of analysing how businesses compete with each other, economists have developed a theory of **perfect competition**. Perfect competition does not exist in a pure form in the real world because there are always differences between sellers, for example one street vendor of plain-coloured T-shirts might be more friendly than another vendor of identical items.

The idea of perfect competition that economists have modelled is based on the following assumptions:

- There would be lots of firms competing with each other.
- Each firm would produce an identical product.
- Each producer would know exactly what the others were producing and the prices they were charging.
- There would be no barriers to new firms entering the market, and no barriers to exit, so firms could enter or leave the market easily.
- Each firm would produce only a small percentage of the overall production in the market.
- There would be lots of buyers, each of whom would know the prices charged by all the sellers.

Given these conditions, economists believe that:

- businesses would all charge the same price
- this price would be the minimum that a business could charge without going out of business
- the price would just enable each business to cover its costs and to make the minimum (normal) profit required to keep operating in the market
- no firm would risk charging more than the market price, because they would make no sales if they did so.

### Price takers

Firms operating under perfect competition would charge the market price. They are thus price takers rather than price makers.

## Monopoly

A monopoly is the opposite of perfect competition. In a pure monopoly there is only one firm in an industry, so there is no competition. There are very few pure monopolies in the real world, but there are local examples, for example there may be only a single shop in a remote area. There are businesses that are so large that they can benefit from the same advantages as monopolies, for example Microsoft, which provides the operating system for most computers. Microsoft is able to use its virtual monopoly position to create exclusive deals with computer manufacturers.

In some countries government-owned corporations have monopoly powers. For example, state-owned oil companies sometimes manage all the oil reserves in that country.

### Price makers

One of the main features of a monopoly is that it acts as a price maker. A price maker chooses what price to charge rather than having to charge a price that is identical or very similar to the prices charged by rivals. Microsoft, mentioned above, is able to choose the price it charges to computer manufacturers, although of course it would not want to make this price unaffordable to the manufacturers.

### The demand curve for a monopolist

Monopolists are faced with a highly inelastic demand curve. As a result, when monopolists raise prices they tend to lose a relatively small number of sales (Figure 3.13.1).

### The features of a monopoly

A monopoly has the following market characteristics:

- There is only one firm and it controls the market.
- It is almost impossible for new firms to enter the market.
- The monopolist is a price maker, setting the market price.
- Monopolists make abnormal levels of profit.
- Because monopolists control the market, they can restrict the quantity of goods they supply in order to raise prices and make abnormal profit.

Examples of virtual monopolies include Microsoft Internet Explorer for accessing the internet, and Google for carrying out internet searches.

### KEY POINTS

- Perfect competition involves intense competition between many firms, leading to price taking.
- Monopoly consists of just one firm in the market. The monopolist sets the market price.

### SUMMARY QUESTIONS

1 Why do all firms in a perfectly competitive market need to charge the same price?

2 What would happen if the firms tried to charge a higher price?

3 Are monopoly firms able to set prices? Give a reason for your answer.

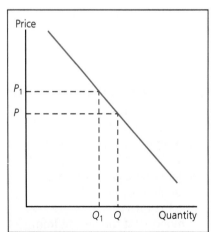

**Figure 3.13.1** An inelastic demand curve for a monopolist

# Oligopoly and monopolistic competition

Airline routes to the Caribbean are dominated by a small number of airlines

## Market structures in the real world

Perfect competition only exists as a model created by economists to identify the characteristics of intense competition. Monopolies do exist in the real world, for example when the government is responsible for water supply and electricity, or one private firm has cornered the market. However, most markets have the combined features of monopoly market structures and competitive structures. Economists have therefore analysed two other forms of market structure that are closely representative of how businesses compete with each other in the real world: **oligopoly** and **monopolistic competition**.

### Oligopoly

Oligopoly means 'competition between a few producers'. Many markets on a global, regional, national and local scale are dominated by a few suppliers. For example, many airline routes to the Caribbean are dominated by just a small number of airlines. If you wanted to travel between Bridgetown and London (not necessarily direct) you would have to choose from Air Canada, Caribbean Airlines, Virgin Atlantic, British Airways or American Airlines. Although there are only a few suppliers, the competition between these airlines can be intense. They will compete with each other in a number of ways, for example by price, service, reliability or the days on which they operate.

The market structure of oligopoly markets consists of the following features:

• There are only a few firms in the market.

• Barriers to entry and exit are high, often because of economies of scale. The few firms that dominate the industry may employ expensive technologies.

• Products offered may be very similar or they may be differentiated.

• Firms tend to be price setters rather than price takers. However, there may be a market leader whose prices other firms tend to copy.

| CASE STUDY | Bananas and the oligopoly market |
| --- | --- |

World banana production is dominated by an oligopoly market structure. In 2010 five global companies accounted for 87 per cent of the global export market for bananas. While in the Caribbean bananas are grown by small independent growers, in Central America and increasingly in Africa and Asia they are grown by national banana companies and large growers. The five large transnational companies, Dole, Chiquita, Del Monte, Fyffes and Noboa, dominate the way that bananas are grown, distributed and sold. They are able to exploit economies of scale to dominate the market. Small independent growers that want to sell to the international market have to accept prices dictated to them by the large multinationals.

### Questions

**1** What are the market characteristics of the global banana market?

**2** Are businesses operating in this market price takers or price setters?

## Monopolistic competition

Monopolistic competition exists where many competing producers are selling products that are differentiated from each other. Products are substitutes for each other but they have differences of brand and different features. In the short run a firm can make abnormal profits because of this differentiation. However, in the longer term new firms can enter the industry attracted by these profits, so abnormal profits will be competed away.

The market structure under monopolistic competition has the following features:

* There are many producers and consumers, and no individual firm can control the market price.
* Consumers believe that there are differences between the products being offered by the firms competing in the market.
* There are few barriers to entry and exit from the market.
* Producers have some control over the prices they charge in the short period.

Producers often gain more market control, and so more monopolistic power, by applying for patents or trademarks. A patent is a grant provided by the official patent office giving the creator of an invention the sole right to apply it. A trademark is the exclusive right of one party, such as a business, to apply a word, phrase, symbol or design that is protected in law.

## Profits in different market structures

* Monopolists can make abnormal profits in the short and long periods.
* Oligopolists can make abnormal profits in the short and long periods.
* Monopolistic competitors can make abnormal profits in the short period but not in the long period.
* Perfect competitors can make abnormal profits in the short period but only normal profit in the long period.

# Market failure

Inoculating children against harmful diseases not only benefits the children, but the whole community too

## What is market failure?

When the market uses resources well to give consumers what they want, economists say that there is market efficiency. When markets fail to create economic efficiency, market failure occurs. This happens when markets:

- fail to produce goods that consumers want
- fail to use resources efficiently
- fail to produce the quantities of goods required
- fail to produce goods at acceptably low prices
- lead to negative externalities (see below).

A good example of market failure relates to the provision of treatment for children with HIV and AIDS. Large numbers of children, particularly in poorer countries, are born with HIV/AIDS contracted from their mothers. These children are in desperate need of drugs. The price of these medicines, however, is too high for most families. The market therefore fails these children.

## Causes of market failure

The following are the most common causes of market failure:

- Monopoly: in 3.13 we saw that monopolists can raise the price and limit the quantity they supply to the market in order to maximise their profits. The market thus fails some consumers who are not able to pay the monopolist's prices. For example, some airline routes between smaller Caribbean islands are controlled by a monopoly airline. Prices are often too high for many people. Another example is Cable and Wireless, which lost its exclusive telecommunications licence in Barbados because the government wanted to open the market to other companies.

- Public goods and merit goods: the market system will often fail to supply goods described as **public goods** (essential goods and services that benefit the wider public, such as street lighting, good roads, a police force and fire service). Individuals might be reluctant to pay for these services because people who choose not to pay (free-riders) would still benefit from them. It is very difficult to get the people who benefit to pay for them. Public goods therefore have to be provided by the government, which usually funds them by means of taxes. A **merit good** is one with substantial benefits (sometimes referred to as **positive external effects** or **externalities**) for society as a whole rather than being restricted to individuals. Everyone benefits if merit goods are provided at low cost, but the market might not provide merit goods, for example inoculation against a particular disease.

- Positive/negative externalities, including pollution: the market often ignores or hides the negative costs to society of economic activities. For example, bananas grown on large Central American plantations are cheaper than those produced by smallholders in the Caribbean. However, Central American producers use large quantities of agrochemicals in growing the bananas. Employees living in housing on the plantations are exposed to these chemicals; spraying often takes place while they are working in the fields. The result is air and water pollution and long-term damage to the land. When the land can no longer support banana production, new plantations are developed, destroying tropical rainforest. The market thus supports inefficient and harmful production, and fails to take account of the positive externalities of many activities. (By contrast, small-scale organic agricultural production encourages biodiversity, which benefits both local people and ecotourists.)

## Government intervention

Making a failing market more efficient will make society better off. Market failure therefore provides a justification for government intervention. Governments may intervene to break up monopolies by encouraging competitors to enter a market. They can also use taxes to penalise businesses that abuse the market, for example by taxing companies that create pollution.

There may also be too much government interference in the market. Economists identify this as government failure. An example might be government taxes that are so high that they discourage business activity that could be beneficial to society.

**EXAM TIP**

Make sure that you can define market failure, and give reasons for it. It occurs when the market fails to lead to economic efficiency and can arise from monopoly activity, the nature of public goods and the existence of externalities.

**KEY POINTS**

- Market failure arises when the market fails to deliver economic efficiency.
- Causes of market failure stem from the actions of monopolists, the failure to account for externalities, and the nature of public and merit goods.

**SUMMARY QUESTIONS**

1 Explain in your own words what you understand by 'market failure'.

2 Give examples of market failures in your country.

# The consequences of market failure

Pollution to the environment is a substantial market failure

**EXAM TIP**

You should be able to distinguish between the causes of market failure (e.g. monopoly power, information asymmetry) and the effects, that are concerned with the resulting inefficiency of the failure. Although specific individuals (e.g. the monopolist) might benefit, society as a whole loses out. By tackling market failure it is possible to create solutions that increase society's prosperity.

## The macro and micro markets

Markets often fail society by not working so as to reduce economic problems, for example protecting people from unemployment or from the harmful effects of pollution. The consequences of market failure can be identified at both a **macro-economic** (large-scale) and a **micro-economic** (small-scale) level. These are the two main levels at which economists examine the economy.

The macro-economy consists of all of the economic units that make up the overall economy – that is, all the firms and all the consumers. When there is inefficiency in the economy as a whole, there will be macro-economic problems – unemployment, for example.

The micro-economy is concerned with small-scale interactions, for example studying the pricing policy of an individual firm. An example of micro-economic market failure might be a situation in which an individual firm fails to operate in an efficient way. A monopolist might contribute to inefficiency by restricting supply and/or raising prices so that resources are not used as effectively as they would be in a more competitive market structure.

### Examples of market failure at a macro level

Markets fail when they are unable to allocate resources efficiently. Both the economy and society suffer the consequences. The following are some examples of such consequences:

• Pollution: the market may not fully take into account the cost of waste, which can result in the inefficient production of pollution as a by-product of economic activity.

• Unemployment: this can happen when wages are higher than the level required to create full employment. Unemployment leads to a range of social and economic problems, particularly when levels are high and sustained over several years.

• Retrenchment (cutting back – a frequent consequence): as a result of failing demand in the economy, firms might start to make cut-backs. They reduce their own expenditure, with a knock-on effect on other businesses, which then face falling demand of their own.

• Economic depression: this occurs when there is a general fall in demand that is widely felt across the economy. It typically follows a period of retrenchment.

• Increase in poverty: this can result from the failure of the economy to allocate resources efficiently. An efficient economy allocates resources to meet customer requirements, but when the market fails significant numbers of people can find that they are living in poverty.

• A decline in the provision for the welfare of society: macro-economic failure results in the inability of businesses to generate wealth and pay taxes. The government takes in less in tax revenue, so is less able to provide welfare benefits for people who need them.

Because of the consequences of market failure at a macro-economic level, there is a strong argument for governments to take action to control some of these failures. They can do this by taxing pollution and providing welfare benefits to poor people for example.

## Micro-economic market failure

Micro-economic failure takes place at the level of small-scale interactions with the economy. For example, an individual firm may take advantage of a local monopoly to charge high prices and restrict the supply of goods. A trade union may restrict the supply of labour and raise wages, so that some potential employees cannot get jobs.

> **DID YOU KNOW?**
>
> The consequences of market failure can be illustrated through taxi services: the fare that you pay for the journey does not fully take into account the pollution caused by the taxi and the harmful effects on the environment. If you had to pay the full cost of the environmental cost of the journey, you might make fewer such journeys.

> **KEY POINTS**
>
> • The market often fails both at macro and micro levels.
> • As a consequence of market failure there are a range of inefficiencies, such as the creation of pollution and the failure to tackle problems such as poverty and unemployment.

> **SUMMARY QUESTIONS**
>
> 1 Who loses out when markets fail? Give some examples from your local community or from your country.
>
> 2 What is the difference between macro- and micro-economic failure?
>
> 3 List four groups of people who may suffer from market failure, providing examples of situations where they would lose out.

> **DID YOU KNOW?**
>
> Some pharmaceutical companies are accused of failing the market by restricting the supply of medicines and drugs in order to keep the price high for richer consumers. Poorer consumers then cannot afford to buy some essential medicines.

> **EXAM TIP**
>
> When considering market failure, think about who the market is failing. Motorists playing very loud music in the car may feel that they are consuming resources efficiently, but passers-by (society) may be disturbed by the noise pollution and feel that this is not a desirable (efficient) use of resources.

# Section 3    Practice exam questions

## SECTION 1: Multiple-choice questions

1 What does a typical supply curve show about the relationship between the amount supplied of a product and its price?

  a   Firms will supply more at a lower price

  b   Consumers will buy more at a higher price

  c   Firms will supply more at a higher price

  d   Consumers will buy more at a lower price

2 A key benefit of the market is that:

  a   It enables the government to set prices for goods

  b   Prices help to signal to producers what goods to supply

  c   It helps to raise prices to the benefit of suppliers

  d   It is centrally coordinated by planning authorities

3 Which of the following factors will cause a shift to the right in the demand curve for MP3 players?

  a   An increase in the price of MP3 players

  b   A fall in incomes

  c   A rise in the price of substitutes for MP3 players

  d   A fall in the price of substitutes for MP3 players

4 A movement down a demand curve is called:

  a   An extension in demand

  b   A contraction in demand

  c   An increase in price

  d   A fall in demand

5 Which of the following is least likely to result in an increase in the price of oil?

  a   A decline in known oil reserves

  b   Hurricane activity stopping oil-pumping activity

  c   Increases in the demand for oil

  d   Improved oilfield productivity

6 The demand for sugar on a global scale is increasing. The effect on the world sugar market of a reduction in sugar cane production in the Caribbean is likely to be:

  a   An increase in the price of sugar

  b   An increase in the demand for sugar

  c   An increase in the supply of sugar

  d   None

7 The elasticity of demand for petrol is measured as $-\frac{1}{2}$. This means that:

  a   A fall in the price of petrol will lead to a proportional increase in the quantity demanded for petrol

  b   The demand for petrol is inelastic

  c   A rise in the cost of producing petrol by $1 will lead to a $2 increase in the price of petrol

  d   A rise in the price of petrol by 10 per cent will lead to a 20 per cent fall in the quantity demanded for petrol

8 Which of the following describes a situation where demand for a good is income elastic?

  a   Income increases by 20 per cent while demand for the good increases by 18 per cent

  b   Demand for the good increases by a smaller proportion than the change in income

  c   Demand for a good increases by a greater proportion than the change in income

  d   Demand for a good increases by 10 per cent while income increases by 10 per cent

9 In which of the following situations would a firm be a price setter while having to compete with many other sellers?

  a   Monopoly

  b   Oligopoly

  c   Monopolistic competition

  d   Perfect competition

10 Which of the following market structures best describes the global export market for bananas?

  a  Monopoly

  b  Oligopoly

  c  Monopolistic competition

  d  Perfect competition

11 A situation where quantity supplied exceeds quantity demanded at a given price is one in which there is:

  a  Shortage          b  Surplus

  c  Market equilibrium   d  Excess demand

12 Which of the following is an indication of market failure?

  a  Efficient use of resources

  b  Firms supplying goods that consumers want

  c  Negative externalities

  d  Acceptably low prices

## SECTION 2: Structured questions

1 a  Define (i) demand (ii) supply. (*4 marks*)

  b  With the aid of a diagram, explain the effect of a fall in the price of television sets on the quantity of television sets supplied to the market. (*6 marks*)

  c  Describe three determinants of the demand for rice. (*3 marks*)

  d  Explain one factor that would lead to an increase in the supply of rice to the market. (*2 marks*)

2 a  Draw illustrations and describe the two laws of demand. (*6 marks*)

  b  Draw a diagram and explain what would happen if the supply of cement to the construction market increases while demand remains the same. (*6 marks*)

  c  Give an example of how the concept of *ceteris paribus* might be applied. (*3 marks*)

3 a  Describe two situations in which the conditions of demand will change. (*4 marks*)

  b  Illustrate a situation in which the conditions of demand for a product improve. (*3 marks*)

  c  Illustrate the impact when the government:

    i  raises the subsidy on the production of a crop (*4 marks*)

    ii  raises taxes by a set percentage per unit of sales of a good. (*4 marks*)

4 a  Define market equilibrium. (*2 marks*)

  b  Draw a diagram to illustrate a situation where the demand for a good increases while supply remains the same. Show the impact on the market equilibrium. Explain your diagram. (*8 marks*)

  c  Define inelastic demand. (*2 marks*)

  d  Give three reasons to explain why the price elasticity of some goods is higher than that of others. (*6 marks*)

  e  Explain why a good of your choice has a high cross elasticity with one or more other goods. (*2 marks*)

5 a  Identify two market structures in which there is a high level of competition between rival firms. (*2 marks*)

  b  Explain the key features of one of these markets in terms of numbers of buyers and sellers, freedom of market entry and price controls. (*6 marks*)

  c  How can some firms operate as 'price makers'? (*3 marks*)

  d  Give three reasons for market failure. (*6 marks*)

  e  Describe three consequences of market failure at a macro level. (*3 marks*)

# 4 The financial sector

## 4.1
# The role of the financial sector

The function of the Trinidad central bank is to supervise the financial system

## The financial sector

In a modern economy many transactions take place on a credit basis. At the same time individuals, companies and institutions borrow and lend money so that transactions can be made. The financial sector is the sector of the economy that makes all this possible. The financial sector consists of:

- financial institutions, for example banks and credit unions
- financial instruments, for example loans, cheques and cash
- a regulatory framework – that is, rules and laws governing financial transactions.

## Financial institutions

Financial intermediaries are organisations whose main task is to channel funds between institutions, lenders and borrowers. Savers (lenders) deposit their savings with a financial intermediary which then lends those funds to borrowers (Figure 4.1.1).

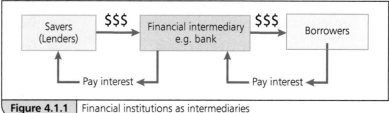

**Figure 4.1.1** | Financial institutions as intermediaries

Financial institutions may also lend money through a financial market. Examples of financial institutions include:

- high street banks (commercial banks) – take deposits from customers and lend them to other customers or to business (see 4.2)
- investment banks – use funds deposited with them to invest long term in companies
- building societies – lend funds for the purchase of houses, buildings and land (see 4.4)
- credit unions – cooperative financial institutions owned and controlled by their members (see 4.3)

- pension funds – companies that collect savings from people when they are younger and pay out funds to these people when they reach retirement age
- insurance companies – enable businesses and households to have risks and losses covered in return for a regular payment of a premium (see 4.4).

## Financial instruments

The financial sector creates a range of **financial instruments** to enable savings, borrowing and transactions. For example, a saver can open a savings account with a commercial bank into which they make regular payments and receive interest on the sum deposited in their account. A borrower can take out a loan, usually for a fixed period, for example 5 years, on which they will pay interest. Financial institutions such as banks also create a range of financial instruments for making transactions, such as cheques and credit cards.

## Regulation of financial institutions

The financial sector needs to be carefully regulated by the government and the central bank. Regulation covers such issues as:

- who can set up a financial institution
- the amount of funds that the financial institution must hold to cover withdrawals or debts
- how much the financial institution can lend and to whom
- how much interest financial institutions can charge.

## Central banks

Many individual countries, including Jamaica, Trinidad, Barbados and Guyana, have a **central bank**. There is also the Eastern Caribbean Central Bank which serves several countries. The job of a central bank is to supervise the financial system of a particular country or group of countries. The head of the central bank holds regular meetings with senior officials from the other banks and other lending institutions to outline the policy for lending. If there is too much spending in the economy, the central bank will ask financial institutions to cut their lending. The central bank is also responsible for:

- printing notes and minting the coins
- setting interest rates, by establishing at what rate it will lend to other financial institutions; the central bank is the lender of last resort – it will lend to a financial institution if they need cash in an emergency
- supervising monetary policy – this determines the amount of money in the economy as well as the interest rate
- acting as banker for the commercial banks
- looking after government tax revenues and helping the government to borrow money.

**KEY POINTS**

- Financial intermediaries help to channel savings from borrowers into loans.
- The financial sector consists of financial institutions, financial instruments and the regulatory framework.
- Central banks play a key role in regulating the financial sector.

**SUMMARY QUESTIONS**

1 What role do financial intermediaries play in financial markets?

2 Explain four key points of difference between a central bank and a commercial bank.

# The functions of the financial sector

The three largest banks in Trinidad manage over 70 per cent of bank assets

## EXAM TIP

Make sure you can explain how the financial sector helps the smooth running of the economy. Government, businesses and households need a safe place to store their wealth and also a means to gain credit. The financial sector performs these functions.

## Functions of the financial sector

The financial sector, which is important in the Caribbean, as elsewhere, manages the bank accounts and credit requirements of citizens within the region. It also provides government, businesses and consumers with credit. The financial sector is responsible additionally for managing the pensions and insurance needs of Caribbean citizens. A number of Caribbean countries are also centres for offshore banking: they are the base for overseas financial institutions managing the deposits, investments and transactions of foreign nationals.

| CASE STUDY | The financial sector in Trinidad |
|---|---|

Trinidad has one of the most highly developed financial sectors in the Caribbean. There is considerable concentration in this sector. For example, the three largest banks manage over 70 per cent of bank assets. Of the eight banks operating in Trinidad, six of them are foreign-owned. The banks engage in a range of activities, from handling customer accounts to providing business loans, and even managing pension arrangements for customers. The three largest insurance companies transact over 75 per cent of the insurance business in Trinidad. Because the financial sector is so well developed in Trinidad, the island's banks, insurance companies and other financial institutions also do a lot of business in other parts of the Caribbean.

As well as insurance companies and banks, Trinidad also has pension funds, credit unions (see 4.3) and unit trusts. The financial sector is so complex that the Central Bank of Trinidad and Tobago is responsible for regulating it so that the public can have confidence in these financial institutions. The central bank is also responsible for regulating offshore banks owned by foreign companies to make sure that they are carrying out their business in a lawful and responsible way.

### Questions

**1** What are the main institutions that make up Trinidad's financial sector?

**2** What are the main functions of the financial sector in Trinidad?

**3** To what extent does the financial sector in Trinidad play an international role?

### Lending

The first function of the financial sector therefore is to provide funds for governments, businesses and individuals to borrow. This helps the economy to run smoothly. The government can borrow money to finance projects such as building schools and hospitals. Businesses can borrow money to invest in new buildings and capital, and to provide short-term cash to make pressing payments. Households can borrow money to finance capital expenditures such as house building or so that they have the means to buy goods, paying the loans back to the bank at a later date.

## Investment advice

Financial institutions play a major role in providing investment and other financial advice. When an individual or business makes an investment they are taking a risk – that is, putting in money, with the return expected depending on how much risk they are prepared to take. Advisors working for investment and commercial banks are experienced in managing risk and give information to investors about different investment opportunities. They also provide advice about how to invest in a pension and different types of insurance.

## Deposits

An important function of financial institutions is to look after the money deposits of customers. Banks in the Caribbean offer a range of different types of savings account. Typically the greater the amount that a customer is willing to deposit, the greater the rate of interest they will receive. There are many different savings schemes, including those for small savers, large savers, older people and junior savers (young people).

## The rate of interest

The rate of interest is the price of borrowing money. Figure 4.2.1 shows factors affecting the rate of interest.

| 0.5% 1% 2% 3% 4% 5% 6% 7% 8% 9% 10% 11% 12% 15% 20% 25% 30% | |
| --- | --- |
| Low interest rate | High interest rate |
| Low-risk investment project | High-risk investment project |
| Short-term loan | Long-term loan |
| Borrower has a good credit history | Borrower has a bad credit history |

**Figure 4.2.1** Factors affecting the rate of interest

## Other functions

Other functions of financial institutions include ensuring liquidity in the economy – that is, providing people and businesses with means of making payments, through bank loans for example. Financial institutions like insurance companies also help businesses and individuals with risk reduction, reducing their exposure to risk. For example, insurance companies will provide compensation for some losses that individuals and businesses incur.

### KEY POINTS

- The main function of the financial sector is to provide loans and other forms of credit to businesses, governments and households.
- Other functions include managing pensions and insurance and giving investment advice.

### SUMMARY QUESTION

In the financial sector:

a What are the key functions?

b Who sets interest rates?

c Who benefits from interest rates?

d Who pays interest, and why?

# The informal sector

The Communal Co-operative Credit Union is one of the best known in Grenada

## Definition of the informal sector

The informal sector consists of economic activities that are not officially regulated and which take place outside the formal norms of business transactions.

The importance of the informal sector lies in the fact that for many households and firms it provides their only source of access to credit. This is particularly true for low-income households and for small business owners who are setting up for the first time.

## Reasons for the existence of the informal sector

Throughout the world there is a division between those with access to financial institutions and those without. Typically financial institutions prefer to deal with people who have a steady income and a proven record of paying back credit. As a result it is more difficult for those who may have irregular incomes, for example seasonal workers, to make use of financial services from the formal sector.

Another reason for the development of the informal sector is that it is more convenient for people living in remote locations away from towns and cities.

## Credit unions

Credit unions are set up to encourage saving. They also provide credit at competitive rates to their members. Some credit unions are very small with just a few members, while others are multi-billion-dollar enterprises.

The main characteristic that distinguishes a credit union from a bank is that the members are the owners of the organisation and use a one-person-one-vote system to elect a board of directors. The board then decides on policies such as how much interest to charge on loans.

Larger credit unions have many features in common with banks, such as savings accounts, chequing accounts and credit cards. Many people in the Caribbean are members of credit unions, particularly in Dominica and Barbados. In Trinidad and Tobago credit unions are such an important source of financial services that there are regulations governing their setting up and running.

For many years credit unions were an important part of the informal sector, but in most areas they are now part of the formal sector. To be part of the formal sector they have to be registered and their activities are regulated. They are defined by The World Council of Credit Unions as 'not-for-profit cooperative institution[s]'.

**CASE STUDY** | The Communal Co-operative Credit Union

The Communal Co-operative Credit Union is one of the best-known and most highly respected credit unions in Grenada. It was set up in 1964 with just 100 members who each put in $500. To become a member of the union and open a savings account, you need to purchase 40 shares at $5 each. Members make regular savings and are able to take out loans for sensible and productive activities. These might include loans to make house or furniture purchases, to pay for a wedding or a child's education. The credit union also provides savings accounts for children so that they acquire the habit of saving early.

Being a member of the credit union also provides benefits such as being able to buy goods at a discount in many shops in Grenada, as well as entitling all members to a dividend at the end of the year. The Credit Union is a not-for-profit organisation, so any surplus that is made is either ploughed back into improving the credit union or given as a dividend to members.

### Questions

1 What do you think are the principal differences between the Communal Co-operative Credit Union and a commercial bank?

2 What are the main functions of the Credit Union?

### Pawning

Pawning means giving up an item, usually of value, as a pledge against a loan. If borrowers fail to make repayments on the loan at the agreed time, they may lose the item pledged. Pawning gold jewellery may enable a person to raise sufficient funds to ease short-term liquidity requirements. Pawning is an important part of the informal sector in the Caribbean.

**DID YOU KNOW?**

Many credit unions are directed by a volunteer board, whose directors are not compensated for their services. Credit unions are also non-profit-making. Very often the unions were set up by groups of people with a shared interest to support each other, for example members of a church.

**KEY POINTS**

- The informal financial sector consists of unregulated organisations.
- Increasingly today parts of the informal financial sector are being regulated.

**EXAM TIP**

Although today credit unions are typically part of the formal sector of the economy, remember that their roots and development were in the non-regulated informal sector.

**SUMMARY QUESTIONS**

1 Explain what is meant by an *informal sector*.

2 Why does an informal financial sector exist in Caribbean economies?

# Other financial institutions

## Some important financial institutions

In 4.7 to 4.9 the work of the most important financial institutions – the central bank, the commercial banks and the stock exchange – will be considered. In 4.4 we examine some of the other financial institutions (Figure 4.4.1).

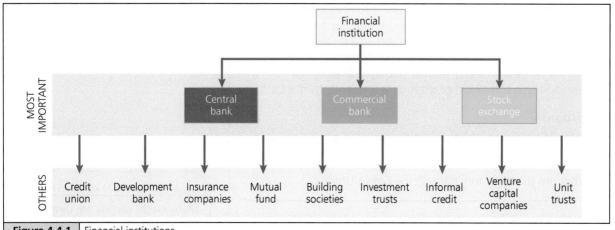

**Figure 4.4.1** | Financial institutions

Each of the financial institutions examined in 4.4 helps the economy to run more smoothly, whether by providing loans for capital projects (for example from development banks or mutual funds) or covering risks (for example from insurance companies).

### Development banks

A development bank is an institution that uses its funds for development purposes. In Trinidad and Tobago there is the Agricultural Development Bank, but perhaps the best-known development bank with the widest responsibility is the Caribbean Development Bank. It came into existence in 1970 with $50 million of capital. Its purpose is to support the economic development of the Caribbean region, particularly remote communities, and to help tackle poverty. The offices of the Bank are in St Michael, Barbados. The Bank consists of two types of member:

• regional members – that is, Caribbean economies
• non-regional members, including Canada, the UK and China.

There are 21 regional members and they are referred to as Borrowing Member Countries. These regional members own the bank. The members contribute capital and regional members have 60 per cent of the shares in the bank. The bank can also borrow capital internationally. It lends to governments and businesses for specific projects, such as for agriculture, marketing, mining, education and housing. The bank also helps out economies in times of natural disaster.

## Building societies

Building societies were originally set up by groups of investors to pool funds to build houses. Building societies are owned by their members. Savers can deposit money to earn interest. They can then borrow from the building society to buy property or land. Borrowers take out a mortgage for a given period, for example 20 years, during which time they repay the sum, with interest. The building society holds the deeds (legal title) to the property until the final payment is made. Building societies offer a wide range of financial services, such as savings and chequing (current) accounts, and insurance.

## Mutual funds and investment trusts

Mutual funds and investment trusts are similar. Savers make small investments and the mutual or investment trust reinvests these in a range of shares and other financial assets. The managers of the fund or trust use their professional expertise to invest the money wisely on behalf of the investors, who receive an annual reward or dividend. These institutions help to channel funds from small investors to companies and other borrowers requiring funds. A mutual fund is open-ended: its capital will expand as new members join the fund and existing investors put in more capital. Members can also sell back their share to the fund.

Investment trusts are closed-ended: they start with a fixed pot of investments and issue a certain amount of capital. Investors in the trust will then sell the units of investment that they hold on the stock exchange.

## Insurance companies

An insurance company manages risks for its customers – businesses and households with risks that they want the insurance company to cover on their behalf. Companies can insure against this risk by taking out a policy that sets out details of the conditions under which the insurance company will pay compensation. The insured customer will need to pay a regular premium to the insurance company.

Insurance companies cover a range of risks, from fire damage, flooding and personal accident to risks specific to businesses, such as employer's liability (accidents to employees) and public liability (damages to members of the public caused by the company). Insurance companies operating in the Caribbean include Guardian Life, Sagicor, NCB, Clico and British American.

## Informal credit institutions

There are a number of informal credit institutions operating in the Caribbean, such as sou sou and meeting turns. Each member of a meeting turn (a 'hand') pools an equal sum of money over a set period (say $100 per month). At the end of the period one person receives all the money pooled. Members take turns until everyone has had at least one 'turn' or hand, and received the lump sum. This is an excellent way for a group of friends or colleagues to save and is very useful for people who may not have access to a credit union or bank.

**DID YOU KNOW?**

There are different terms for meeting turns: in some areas they are known as sou sou boxes and in other areas partners or syndicates.

**KEY POINTS**

- Financial institutions provide capital for business and help to cover business risks.
- The Caribbean Development Bank, building societies, investment trusts and mutual funds all provide capital for investment projects.

**SUMMARY QUESTION**

Explain the difference between

a a development bank and a commercial bank

b an insurance company and a building society

c a sou sou and a mutual fund.

# The importance of money

For centuries cowrie shells were used as money in many parts of the world

## What is money?

Money is anything that is widely accepted or used to exchange for goods. Today when we think about money we are typically referring to notes and coins. However, households and businesses also use many other ways of making payments, such as credit and debit cards.

### The development of money

Before money was used, people would barter – that is, exchange goods for goods, say a goat for several chickens. This requires the two people who make the trade to want what the other has to offer (a double coincidence of wants). The obvious disadvantage is that one partner may not have enough goods to make the exchange fair, or they might not want a whole goat, for example. People realised that small but valuable items, such as cowrie shells, could be used instead.

Over time people began to use precious metals such as gold and silver as a means of exchange. The next step was for coins to be developed. Typically these coins would be minted from metals such as silver and copper. Particular geographical areas would develop their own coinage. To gain recognition and acceptability the coins would be stamped, for example with a picture of a known ruler, such as an emperor.

The origins of banking go back thousands of years to the time when merchants would lend money to purchase land or seed, for example. Modern banking as we know it began in Italy in the 14th century, when rich merchant families started to operate from fixed premises and opened up branches in other parts of the world in which they traded. As commercial banking spread across the globe, banks started to make loans to customers. New ways of paying developed, such as bank notes (easier to carry than bags of coins), and eventually cheques, which evolved from early bank notes. These notes were promises by the bank to pay to the holder of the note a given sum of money in return for the note. As confidence grew in notes, banks started to print them in convenient units such as $10 and $50.

Since the late 20th century banking has been transformed by the development of electronic communications. Today 'money' consists of coins, notes and cheques and card transactions as well as electronic banking, where customers can pay for goods online. Large businesses carry out many of their transactions online.

Table 4.5.1 summarises the stages in the development of money.

**Table 4.5.1** Stages in the development of money

| | |
|---|---|
| 1 | Commodities, e.g. cowrie shells, are used as money |
| 2 | Scarce metal, e.g. silver, is used as money |
| 3 | Money takes the form of coins |
| 4 | Development of paper money |
| 5 | Modern forms of money: cheques, card payments, electronic transfer |

## The functions of money

The functions of money are as follows:

- As a medium of exchange: money is generally accepted as a means of payment for most goods.
- As a unit of account: the price of an item can be measured in terms of how many units of currency it is worth. For example, a low-quality top may cost $10, a high-quality one may be valued at $100 or more.
- As a store of value: you can save money because it keeps its value. Saving enables use of the money in the future.
- As a standard for deferred payments: borrowers are able to borrow money and pay it back at a future date.

**KEY POINTS**

- Money is anything that is widely accepted as a means of exchange.
- The functions of money are as a medium of exchange, a unit of account, a store of value and a standard for deferred payments.

**SUMMARY QUESTION**

With reference to the currency of your country, explain how it acts as:

a  a store of value

b  a medium of exchange

c  a standard for deferred payments.

**EXAM TIP**

Make sure that you are clear about the difference between the functions of money – that is, the purposes it serves (see 4.5) – and the qualities of money (see 4.6) – that is, the properties that enable it to be used as money.

# The qualities of money

Candidates should be able to:

- describe the qualities of money
- explain the phrase 'the money supply'.

The East Caribbean dollar is pegged against the US dollar to give it stability

## Qualities of money

The reason that cowrie shells and tobacco were used as money in the past is that they had the essential qualities required to be considered as money. The following are the qualities of money:

- Scarcity: shells were valuable because they were relatively scarce.
- Acceptability: people were prepared to accept shells as payment because they knew that they could use them for future trading.
- Portability: the shells could easily be carried for long distances.
- Durability: the shells were hard-wearing and long-lasting.
- Divisibility: valuing an item at say, half a goat, was hardly practicable. Shells, however, could be supplied in various quantities according to the value of the purchase. In modern terms, items can cost millions of dollars or just a few cents, according to value.
- Uniformity: each unit of money is uniform (the same). So one Jamaican dollar has the same appearance as any other Jamaican dollar and is instantly recognisable as such.

| CASE STUDY | The East Caribbean dollar |
|---|---|

The East Caribbean dollar is the currency of eight of the nine members of the Organisation of East Caribbean States – that is, Antigua and Barbuda, Dominica, Grenada, St Kitts and Nevis, St Lucia, St Vincent and the Grenadines, Anguilla, and Montserrat. These states have a combined population of about 600 000. Queen Elizabeth II appears on one side of the coins and also on the bank notes. The value of the East Caribbean dollar is pegged against the US dollar to give it stability. This means that the East Caribbean Bank establishes the value of the East Caribbean dollar in exchange for a US dollar.

Coins are minted in denominations of 1 cent, 2 cents, 5 cents, 10 cents, 25 cents and 1 dollar. Bank notes are printed in units of 5, 20, 50 and 100 dollars. Control of the quantity of notes is supervised by the Eastern Caribbean Central Bank.

### Questions

1 Describe the four main functions of the East Caribbean dollar.

2 Explain how the East Caribbean dollar is scarce, acceptable, portable, durable and divisible.

## The money supply

**Money supply** means the total stock of money in the economy at any one time. This is controlled by the central bank. If there is too much money, prices are likely to rise in line with the increase. Once prices get out of control, citizens may prefer to use something else as money, for example, tobacco and sugar rather than the state's notes and coins.

We have already seen that there are different forms of money, and economists aim to measure the quantity of money in different forms. A narrow definition of money supply might just include coins and notes. However, today people spend money in different ways, such as by making electronic payments directly from their bank account, or by paying for goods with a credit card. It is very important for the central bank to control the quantity of money both in its narrow and broad senses, in order to keep control over price changes in the economy and control spending. This enables the central bank to make sure that money continues to be seen as and to act as a store of value. Printing too much money means that it will lose its quality as a store of value. Figure 4.6.1 illustrates the definitions of money supply. M0, M1 and M2 are used for different definitions of money supply: M0 is a narrow definition whereas M2 is a broad definition.

### EXAM TIP

Make sure you can define M0, M1 and M2.

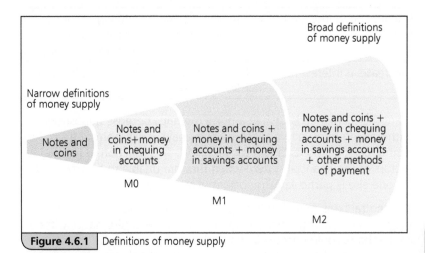

**Figure 4.6.1** | Definitions of money supply

### SUMMARY QUESTION

How does the US dollar possess the following qualities of money in your country: acceptability, scarcity, portability, durability, and divisibility?

### KEY POINTS

- The qualities of money are features of means of payment that help them to be treated as money.
- The money supply is the total stock of money in the economy at any one moment.

# The central bank

## The role of the central bank

The central bank of a country regulates financial activity. The head of the central bank regularly meets with the heads of other financial institutions to outline national policy in relation to lending and other matters.

The work of the central bank of Trinidad and Tobago is representative of the responsibilities of other central banks in the Caribbean. A particularly important role affecting the economy is that of setting the base interest rate. This is the rate on which other banks will base their own interest rates, charging a little more than the base rate.

Changing interest rates helps the central bank to control lending to other banks. The impact of a change in interest rates is shown in Table 4.7.1.

**Table 4.7.1** Effect of changes in interest rates

| Reduction in interest rates | Borrowers find borrowing cheaper, they borrow more, leading to an increase in spending in the economy |
| Increase in interest rates | Savers save more, borrowers borrow less, spending falls |

If another bank needs cash in a hurry (perhaps because depositors are withdrawing unusually large sums of money), it can borrow from the central bank acting as lender of last resort. This function of lending to sectors of the financial system when they are unable to borrow from anyone else is particularly important in a recession.

The central bank may decide to penalise other banks for lending too much and charge them a high rate of interest. Alternatively, the central bank could encourage banks to reduce lending by 'moral suasion'. Other banks set their interest rates at levels just above the central bank's **base rate** or discount rate – that is, the rate set by the central bank on which all other interest rates are based.

**CASE STUDY** | The Central Bank of Trinidad and Tobago

The Central Bank fulfils the following roles:

**Issuing currency:** working with the Ministry of Finance the bank determines the nature of the currency of Trinidad and Tobago, including details of what coins and notes to produce and in what quantities. The bank ensures a sufficient money supply to meet the needs of the economy. It must also make sure that notes and coins are difficult to forge.

**Supervising monetary policy:** the Central Bank works with the Ministry of Finance to create and manage monetary policy, which determines the quantity of money in the economy and the interest rate. Important objectives are to maintain a low and stable rate of inflation and to manage the rate of exchange between the Trinidadian dollar and other foreign currencies.

**Acting as the government's bank:** the bank issues securities in the form of treasury bills and bonds (see 4.10). This enables the government to borrow money. The total amount the government owes to lenders is called the **national debt**. The bills and bonds are official promises to repay money in the future with interest in return for the loan. The bank also manages the government's bank account, settling transactions in the same way a normal bank would do for its customers.

**Acting as banker to the commercial banks:** other banks in Trinidad hold accounts at the Central Bank. Payments between banks can be transferred through their accounts at the Central Bank.

**Managing foreign exchange and the value of the Trinidadian dollar:** the Central Bank licenses other banks and bureaux de change to deal in currencies. The Central Bank seeks to manage the value of the Trinidadian dollar in international markets by buying Trinidadian dollars (using reserves of other trading currencies such as US dollars) if their price is too low and selling them if the price is too high. In theory, since 1993 the Trinidadian dollar has been free to fluctuate against other currencies. In practice, however, the Central Bank controls upward and downward movements in order to create more stability. The Central Bank also holds the national foreign exchange reserves. Reserves of US dollars and other valuable currencies are required to manage international debts and to buy and sell the Trinidadian dollar to keep it stable.

**Regulating the financial sector:** the Central Bank regulates the financial sector, including the banking sector, pension, funds and insurance companies. The Central Bank also licenses all providers of different types of payment system, payment by cheque or credit card. The central bank sets the reserve requirement, that is the percentage of assets that a commercial bank holds in cash or near cash.

**Carrying out economic research and collecting economic statistics:** such information may be about the size of the money supply, or details of the balance of payments between Trinidad and Tobago and the rest of the world (see 6.8).

**As a lender of last resort:** an organisation (the Central Bank) lends to sectors of the financial system when they are unable to borrow from elsewhere. This is particularly important in a recession.

### Question

Which of the roles outlined above involves:

**a** managing the means of payment in the economy

**b** providing banking services to others

**c** managing the Trinidad and Tobago dollar in international markets

**d** maintaining the Trinidad and Tobago dollar as a source of value?

---

**KEY POINTS**

- The central bank has overall responsibility for monetary policy.
- The central bank regulates a country's financial system.
- The central bank prints notes, mints coins and acts as a banker to important institutions.

**SUMMARY QUESTIONS**

1 What are the five most important functions of a central bank?

2 What is the relationship between the central bank and the other banks in a country?

3 What is monetary policy?

**EXAM TIP**

Make sure that you understand the role of the central bank in:

i influencing the macro-economy, for example by setting interest rates and regulating the financial system

ii more specific aspects such as acting as the banker's bank and the government's bank.

# Commercial banks

Commercial banks look after depositors' money, provide loans and enable payments

## What is a commercial bank?

**Commercial banks** provide a safe place to keep money and will also lend money. Sometimes they are called retail banks because their lending to businesses and households is relatively small compared with some investment banks which provide large sums of capital to business.

## The main activities of commercial banks

The basic functions of a bank are:

1 **Keeping money safe**: a bank's vaults are more secure than a safe deposit box in a private house. Individuals and businesses can open bank accounts. They deposit money in the account. Savings accounts pay the depositor a set rate of interest on sums saved. **Current accounts** are for keeping money safe, but sums can be withdrawn to make payments. A current account may pay some interest, but this will be lower than on a savings account. Banks also keep documents and other valuable items in safe deposit boxes.

2 **Lending**: many people and businesses need to borrow money – for example, for expensive purchases such as a car. Businesses may borrow from banks when they want to grow. Borrowing methods include:

- Loans – borrowing a fixed sum (e.g. US$1,000) for a set period of time (e.g. two years). The business will need to pay back the sum borrowed (US$1,000) plus the agreed rate of interest. For example, if the interest rate is 10 per cent, then over the two years the borrower will pay back US$1,100 (US$1,000 + US$100 interest).

- An overdraft – that is, taking out more than has been put into the account. The borrower has an agreed overdraft limit, and will pay interest to the bank if the account is overdrawn.

- Banks offer customers a credit card. This enables users to buy goods and pay for them later. Every month users receive a **statement** showing how much they owe the bank. If they pay the bill by a given date, they will not have to pay interest. However, if they do not pay the bill in full, they are charged a high rate of interest. Many businesses use credit cards to finance short-term cash flow needs. A debit card is a means of payment using funds in your own bank account rather than through borrowing.

- Mortgages – banks lend to firms and households to buy office buildings and factories. The legal deeds of ownership of the property are kept by the bank until the mortgage has been repaid. Mortgages are usually for long periods of time, such as 25 years.

Commercial banks act as financial intermediaries in the way shown in Figure 4.8.1.

## Other banking services

Commercial banks also perform a number of other important services that benefit the economy:

- They provide means of making payment, such as cheques and banker's drafts. These are slips of paper, printed with the name, address and logo of the bank, and customers write in the name of the person and the amount they wish to pay. The bank then transfers money to the recipients. Banks can also make regular payments in the form of standing orders (set payments of regular sums) into a named account. Banks process payments through automatic electronic payments as well as internet banking. In some countries (e.g. in 2018 in the UK) banks will stop the use of cheques because cards are so much easier to use.

- They provide foreign currency. If you visit another country that uses different currency, your local bank may be able to provide you with the currency. However, ATMs (automated teller machines) make it easy for a customer to withdraw money in most urban areas worldwide.

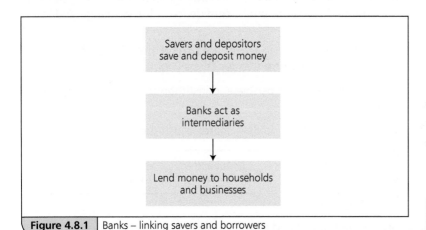

Figure 4.8.1 Banks – linking savers and borrowers

Savers and depositors save and deposit money

Banks act as intermediaries

Lend money to households and businesses

# The stock exchange

Candidates should be able to:

- describe the role of the stock exchange and the share market.

Traders at the Jamaica Stock Exchange are called broker members

**DID YOU KNOW?**

The price of shares depends on how keen buyers are to purchase shares in particular companies. The more popular a share, the higher its price. Investors want to buy shares of companies that make good profits, so that they can take a share of this profit in the form of a dividend and benefit from the rising share price.

**DID YOU KNOW?**

Share prices rise when:

- a company is expected to make good profits
- another company wants to take over the business and is prepared to pay more than the existing share price to complete the deal.

## The stock exchange

The stock exchange was originally a building in which shares in public companies were traded. Many countries now have a stock exchange – a very important institution for raising funds for business. Well-known examples include the New York, London, Mumbai and Beijing Stock Exchanges.

In the Caribbean the principal stock exchanges are the Jamaica, Barbados and Trinidad and Tobago Stock Exchanges, and the Eastern Caribbean Securities Market.

| CASE STUDY | The Jamaica Stock Exchange |
| --- | --- |

The Jamaica Stock Exchange is known as the JSE. It was set up in 1968 and is located at 40 Harbour Street in Kingston. Its governing body has set objectives to promote the orderly development of the highest standards for its members. Its rules are designed to ensure public confidence in the exchange and in public companies.

The people who trade in shares are **broker members** of the exchange. They perform two functions (Figure 4.9.1):

**1** to act as agents for people and institutions wishing to buy and sell shares

**2** to act as principals holding shares which they sell.

| Institutions and individuals wishing to sell shares | → | Traders at the stock exchange | ← | Institutions and individuals wishing to buy shares |
| --- | --- | --- | --- | --- |

| **Figure 4.9.1** | The stock exchange as market place |
| --- | --- |

Shares are bought and sold by broker members on behalf of their clients. Since 2000 the exchange has had an automated trading platform – an electronic system which records and processes all the transactions that are made by the brokers. This enables swift processing and accurate transactions.

For a company to have its shares traded on the JSE it must have a minimum of $200 000 worth of capital and at least half of this must be issued in the form of **ordinary shares**. An ordinary share is a deed (legal document) stating that the holder is a part-owner of a company and entitled to vote at the company annual meeting. Ordinary shareholders are entitled to receive a dividend (reward) for their shares, depending on how much the board of directors of the company decides to allocate to ordinary shareholders. A minimum of 100 shareholders in the company must hold no less than 20 per cent of the ordinary shares that have been issued in the company. Public companies must produce an annual financial statement and circulate it to shareholders.

### Questions

**1** Why might a business want to become a public company and have its shares traded on the stock exchange?

**2** In what ways is the JSE regulated? What is the purpose of this regulation?

## Trading shares

The stock exchange is a market for second-hand shares – that is, shares that a company has already issued. The shares are first issued by a company, for example by offering them for sale to the general public, or by agreeing to have them placed with large financial institutions such as pension funds. The holders of these shares can then have them traded on the stock exchange. Shareholders are rewarded by means of dividends, and by growing demand increasing the price of the shares that they already hold.

## The functions of the stock exchange

The main purpose of the stock exchange is to help public companies raise capital. Financial capital is the money that a business raises from selling shares. The finance can then be used to purchase physical capital, such as buildings and machinery.

The existence of a stock exchange gives the public and financial institutions confidence that:

• they can buy new shares
• they can sell their shares when they want to.

A shareholder in a company is a part-owner of that company. The rewards from holding shares are that:

• every 6 or 12 months shareholders will receive a payment known as a dividend, which is their reward, their share of the company profits
• they may also benefit from the rising value of their shares
• some companies offer special concessions to their shareholders, for example cheap flights for holders of airline shares, or discount vouchers to use in the company's stores.

Shareholders are protected by **limited liability**. This legal protection limits the amount that a shareholder might lose to the value of their shareholding if the company gets into financial difficulty. They would not have to pay more to cover the company's debts. Stock exchanges also protect shareholders with strict rules setting out what a company must do for its shares to be listed on the stock exchange. Listed companies are required to produce an annual report for shareholders and are required to have their accounts checked each year by an independent auditor.

**DID YOU KNOW?**

An institutional investor is an organisation such as a pension fund, unit trust or investment company. It is set up for a particular purpose, which gives it access to large sums of money that it can reinvest. People saving for future pensions pay regular sums into the pension fund and these are then invested on the stock exchange.

**DID YOU KNOW?**

The stock exchange also plays an important role in helping the government to raise finance, through selling bills and bonds. Institutional and other investors lend the government money knowing that they are almost certain to be paid back. In most countries government bonds are more secure than shares in companies, although the return on a government bond may be lower than a dividend on a share in a company.

**KEY POINTS**

• Stock exchanges bring together buyers and sellers through their broker members.
• They enable public companies to raise capital.
• They also help the government to raise finance.

**SUMMARY QUESTIONS**

**1** What work do broker members carry out on a stock exchange?

**2** A stock exchange can be described as 'a market for second-hand shares'. What do you understand by this statement?

# Financial instruments

As a financial instrument, a share certificate represents a binding agreement between two parties

## What is a financial instrument?

A **financial instrument** is a document such as a share certificate or government bond that has a monetary value and represents a binding agreement between two or more parties. Financial instruments are created by a range of financial institutions, and national and local government bodies. The main types of financial instrument are described below.

## Treasury notes and bonds

Governments often need to raise funds for their spending programmes. They therefore issue short-term and long-term financial instruments. A **treasury bill** refers to government borrowing for periods of less than one year. In contrast, **government bonds** are for much longer periods of time, for example 5 or 30 years. Treasury notes promise to repay a fixed sum of money after a given period of time, for example 2, 3, 5 and 10 years. A fixed rate of interest is paid to the holder of these notes. Treasury notes can be bought through a broker at the stock exchange. Interest is typically paid at the end of every 6 months.

The process relating to a 2-year treasury note is set out in Figure 4.10.1.

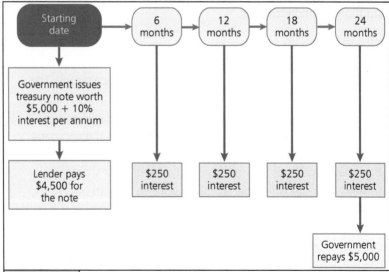

**Figure 4.10.1** How an investor benefits from buying treasury notes

While most government borrowing is for a fixed period, the government also sometimes carries out borrowing with no fixed date for repayment. The holder of this type of government debt would simply earn interest knowing that at some unspecified date in the future their loan will be redeemed.

## Municipal bonds

Municipal bonds work on exactly the same basis as government bonds. The only difference is the borrower. The borrower in the case of municipal bonds is local government rather than national government.

## Corporate bonds

Corporate bonds are similar to other bonds. They are issued by companies as a way of raising money to invest in their business. The bonds will have a face value, for example $100, which is the sum that will be repaid to the investor at a set future date (the redemption date). They pay a set rate of interest each year. Corporate bonds are traded on stock exchanges. When they are first purchased the purchaser will typically pay less than the redemption price for them, for example $80 for a bond to be redeemed in 5 years' time. The closer to the redemption date, the higher the price these bonds will be traded for.

## Equity securities

Equity securities is another name for ordinary shares. The equity capital of a business is the total amount that it raises from selling shares. To own equity means to own shares, and owning a share gives the owner part-ownership of the company. Equities are first issued in given denominations, for example $1 per share, $10 per share. When shares are first issued shareholders will either pay the face value of the share, for example $1.00, less than the face value, for example 90 cents, or more than the face value, for example $1.10. It depends on how good an investment they expect the share to be and how much in dividends they expect to receive. Once a share is issued it is traded on the stock exchange. Over time its price will rise or fall depending on whether investors think that the company is likely to make good or poor profits. A share price in a successful company might rise several times higher than its original face value. If the company wants to raise more capital, it has to apply to the stock exchange to issue more shares.

There is an important distinction between equity financing and debt financing by companies. A company can raise finance internally from its shareholders or by borrowing from a financial institution. The bank rewards shareholders with dividends which depend on the amount of profit it makes. In contrast, its repayments of debts to lenders involve a fixed rate of interest. High debt financing, for example repaying loans, is particularly burdensome in years when profits are low because they have to be repaid. In contrast, a business can elect only to pay shareholders a small dividend in a year of poor profitability. Where companies borrow too much from debt financing they are more likely to get into financial difficulty in periods of recession and when profits are low. Recent financial shocks in the Caribbean and on a global scale have been a major issue for companies that have exposed themselves to too much debt financing rather than raising finance from shareholders.

**EXAM TIP**

Make sure you are familiar with the typical length of different types of bills, bonds and notes and how the holders of these securities are rewarded. You should understand the difference between issue date and redemption date.

**KEY POINTS**

- Government bills are short-term methods of raising finance.
- Municipal bills are used to finance local government projects.
- Corporate bonds and equity shares help a business to raise finance.

**SUMMARY QUESTIONS**

1 Explain the difference between a corporate bond and a municipal bond.

2 Why might a person want to purchase a treasury note?

3 What are equity securities?

# Section 4    Practice exam questions

1  What are the three main tools of monetary policy?

   a  Taxes, subsidies and grants

   b  Taxes, discount rates and the reserve requirement

   c  Discount rates, subsidies and the reserve requirement

   d  Discount rates, the reserve requirement and open market operations

2  Which of the following represents a monetary policy tool?

   a  Taxes

   b  Subsidies

   c  Tariffs

   d  Open market operations

3  The monetary sector in a country is managed by:

   a  The central bank

   b  The commercial bank

   c  The World Bank

   d  The International Monetary Fund

4  A function of a commercial bank is:

   a  Managing the foreign exchange in the country

   b  Lending to the general public

   c  Banker to the government

   d  Banker to foreign central banks

5  Which characteristic of money is closely related to its function as a medium of exchange?

   a  Divisibility

   b  Portability

   c  Acceptability

   d  Durability

6  An institution that encourages thrift among its members is known as:

   a  A commercial bank

   b  A stock exchange

   c  An insurance company

   d  A credit union

7  The central bank stipulates the percentage of a commercial bank's assets that it must hold in liquid form. This is known as the:

   a  Discount rate

   b  Reserve requirement

   c  Total liabilities

   d  Total assets

8  The rate at which the central bank lends to its member banks is known as the:

   a  Savings rate

   b  Lending rate

   c  Interest rate

   d  Discount rate

9  The **main** disadvantage of a barter system is:

   a  The length of time for a transaction

   b  It requires a double coincidence of wants

   c  Establishing a rate of exchange

   d  Production of the good

10  A country's central bank holds a press conference and, to curb inflation, strongly advises the commercial banks to limit the amount of credit available to the general public. This is known as:

   a  Moral suasion

   b  Lender of last resort

   c  Fiscal policy

   d  Paradox of thrift

1 a Define the terms:

    i demand deposit

    ii legal tender. (*4 marks*)

  b List one example of an institution in the informal sector. (*1 mark*)

  c Describe two functions of commercial banks. (*6 marks*)

  d How is moral suasion used to control the money supply? (*4 marks*)

2 a Define the terms:

    i barter

    ii discount rate. (*4 marks*)

  b List one function of the financial sector. (*1 mark*)

  c Describe two functions of a central bank. (*6 marks*)

  d Commercial banks do not print money. Why then do economists say that they can increase the money supply? (*4 marks*)

3 a Define the terms:

    i term deposit

    ii money supply. (*4 marks*)

  b List one characteristic of money. (*1 mark*)

  c Explain two functions of money. (*6 marks*)

  d Differentiate between the lending and saving functions of commercial banks. (*4 marks*)

4 a List three stages in the history of money. (*3 marks*)

  b List four functions of money. (*4 marks*)

  c Explain how open market operations and the reserve requirement can be used to reduce the money supply. (*8 marks*)

  d How does the development of money over time improve the role of the financial sector? (*5 marks*)

5 a Define 'loanable funds'. (*2 marks*)

  b List five characteristics of money. (*5 marks*)

  c Describe four stages in the development of money. (*8 marks*)

  d Explain how treasury bills or bonds are used to decrease the money supply in the economy. (*5 marks*)

# 5 Economic management: policies and goals

## 5.1 The role of government in the economy

### Government responsibility

Nearly all governments take some responsibility for the smooth running of the overall system, the macro-economy. Intervention can be likened to a pilot flying a plane. The pilot watches an instrument panel showing variables such as speed and altitude. The pilot can make adjustments as necessary to make sure that the plane flies smoothly and on course to its destination. So, through their central statistical office, governments receive data about the growth of the economy, the level of inflation (general price changes) and the level of exports and imports. The government minister in charge of the economy assesses the information provided and will decide whether changes to economic policy are necessary.

### Two main policies

There are two main ways in which government can intervene in the economy:

1 Altering interest rates: this is done through the central bank. Reducing interest rates helps to encourage borrowing and spending in the economy. Raising the rates is intended to discourage borrowing and spending and encourage saving. The government can also increase or reduce the quantity of money in the economy. More money encourages more spending; less money reduces spending.

2 Changing the level of the government deficit.

   The government influences the economy:

   • by putting money into the economy through its own spending

   • by taking money out of the economy through taxes.

The relationship between how much the government spends and how much it takes in taxes is very important (Figure 5.1.1). If it spends just as much as it takes, it is said to balance its budget. If it spends less than it takes in taxes it is said to have a surplus budget. When it spends more than it takes in taxes, this is referred to as a **government deficit**. In many countries the government typically runs a government deficit.

**Fiscal policy** refers to deliberate policy by the government to influence the economy through its budget policy. For example, in a period of recession in which there is unemployment in the economy, the

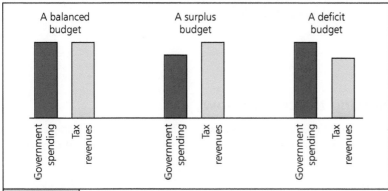

**Figure 5.1.1** Balanced budget, surplus budget and deficit budget

government's fiscal policy may be to have a deficit budget to pump more demand into the economy. In contrast, if there is too much demand in the economy, causing prices to rise, the government might stabilise the economy by running a surplus budget (Figure 5.1.2).

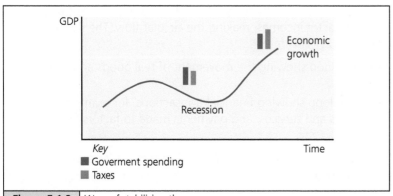

**Figure 5.1.2** Ways of stabilising the economy

## Taxation

A tax is a fee charged by the government on a product, on income or on an activity. Examples of taxes on products are value added taxes levied at each stage in the production of a product. Customs duties are a tax on imported goods. They can be levied at a fixed rate per product, for example 10 cents per item imported, or calculated as a percentage of the value of an import, for example 10 per cent of the import price. Income tax is a tax on a person's income above a certain minimum tax-free amount. Taxes on activities would include taxing a business for the amount of pollution that it creates.

## Government spending

One of the reasons why most countries run a government deficit is because the government spends money so widely. Major items of government expenditure are education, hospitals and public buildings, and infrastructure expenditure on roads, railways and airports.

Government spending also transfers income from one section of the population to another, for example by taxing the rich at a high level and then paying some of this revenue to the poor in the form of welfare benefits: money moved in this way is referred to as transfer payments.

# The circular flow of income

Candidates should be able to:

- explain the circular flow of income
- illustrate the circular flow of income
- explain the terms *national income* and *disposable income*.

Government spending on education is an injection into the circular flow

## Defining the circular flow

The circular flow of income is a way of illustrating relationships in the macro-economy. It assumes that there are two main sets of economic participants:

- households
- firms.

Households own the **factors of production** (land, labour, capital and enterprise). Firms need to use these factors of production. In return firms will pay rewards in the form of factor incomes (rent, wages, interest and profits).

Households then buy the finished goods produced, using the money earned in factor incomes, making the circular flow. The flows shown in Figure 5.2.1 illustrate:

- an inner loop showing the movement of real goods and real factor services
- an outer loop showing financial transactions, for example payment for goods and services, and payments made to factors for their services.

The faster the flow of income, the greater the level of economic output in the economy.

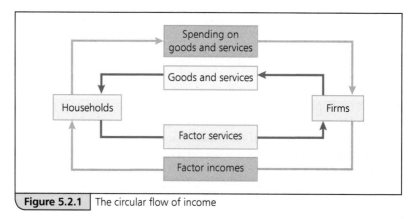

**Figure 5.2.1** The circular flow of income

## National income and disposable income

The total level of income generated by the economy in a particular period of time, for example a year, is referred to as national income or **gross domestic product (GDP)**. However, economists make a distinction between this and **disposable income**. It is important to be clear about this distinction.

Disposable income is the sum that income earners have available to spend in a particular time period. For example, if I receive $100 a week for carrying out a particular job, some of this income will be taken from me in the form of tax. If I am taxed at a rate of 20 per cent, $20 will be taken away from me each week as income tax. My disposable income is thus reduced to $80, the maximum that I can spend from what I receive in my pay packet. (If I then borrow, this would increase my disposable income.)

## More complex circular flow

In reality the circular flow of income is a little more complicated than is indicated in Figure 5.2.1. We should also take account of the role of government and financial institutions.

The government takes money out of the circular flow in the form of taxes. It puts money back into the circular flow in the form of government spending. In 5.1 we saw that when the government spends more than it taxes, there is a deficit budget.

Financial institutions take money out of the circular flow in the form of savings from households. However, this money will typically be put back into the system in the form of loans to businesses for investment. Another major source of injections into the flow of Caribbean economies is remittances from relatives living in the UK and North America.

**DID YOU KNOW?**

When money is withdrawn from the circular flow, this is a *leakage*. There are three leakages: (i) taxes, (ii) savings and (iii) imports of goods from other countries. When money enters the circular flow from outside, this is an *injection*. The three injections are: (i) government spending, (ii) investment and (iii) exports of goods to other countries, bringing in export sales revenues.

Table 5.2.1 Leakages and injections

| Leakages from circular flow | Injections into circular flow |
|---|---|
| Taxes (T) | Government spending (G) |
| Savings (S) | Investment (I) |
| Imports (M) | Exports (X) |

**KEY POINTS**

- The circular flow involves the flow of income and spending between firms and households.
- Financial institutions, government and international trade add injections and take away income in the form of withdrawals from the circular flow.

**SUMMARY QUESTIONS**

1 What are the main flows that take place in the circular flow of income?

2 What flows between households and firms?

3 What is the difference between national income and disposable income?

# GNP and GDP

ECONOMY IN RECESSION GDP FALLING

The press frequently run stories about the rise or fall of national income

## National income

Economic stories in the press and on national radio and television often refer to GDP, GNP or national income. Economists are very interested in the national income because it is a good measure of how successful the economy is in producing goods and services. In fact national income is a measure of three things:

• national output – the total value of all goods produced in the economy (that is, the output of all the industries)

• national income – the total value of all incomes earned in the economy (that is, the total value of factor incomes, rent, wages, profits and interest)

• national expenditure – the total value of all spending in the economy (that is, spending on goods by consumers, business people and government).

These three measures actually all measure the same thing. The economy produces goods, and firms pay factors of production incomes to produce these goods. Households then spend these incomes on the output that is produced (Figure 5.3.1).

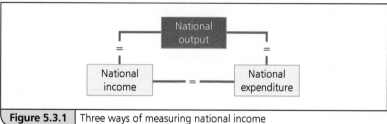

**Figure 5.3.1** Three ways of measuring national income

If national income is rising this means that the economy is producing more goods than in previous periods. As a result incomes will rise and so too will expenditure.

### Gross domestic product

The term you are likely to hear most is gross domestic product (GDP). GDP refers to the total value of the goods produced within a given geographical territory in a given period of time. For example, the GDP of Barbados in 2009 was US$4224 billion.

### Gross domestic product per capita

Gross domestic product per head of population (per capita) is an important economic indicator. The GDP per capita in Barbados in 2009 was US$15 234. To calculate GDP per head, simply divide the GDP of a country by its population.

## Gross national product

Gross national product is defined as the value of goods and services produced in a given time period by factors of production owned within an economy. The GNP of Barbados would include the profits earned by companies from Barbados operating in other parts of the Caribbean and the wider world. It would also include the wages of migrant workers working in other countries and sending their wages home.

**Table 5.3.1** Calculating GDP and GNP

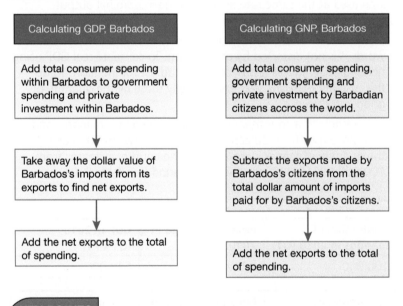

# Measuring output

Candidates should be able to:

• distinguish between nominal output, real output and potential output

• explain the meaning of nominal output, real output and potential output.

The *nominal* value of output of mangos is the value of the mangos in money terms; the *real* value is the value in constant terms

**EXAM TIP**

*Real income is calculated by using the same set of prices in different years. Nominal income uses different prices each year – that is, the prices that prevail in the year for which the nominal income is being calculated.*

## Nominal and real output

There are two main ways of measuring output: nominal and real.

• Nominal output measures output in terms of the value of goods produced in a period of time. For example, the nominal output of a country in 2010 might be measured to be $100 000 worth of goods. In 2011 it might be measured to have increased by $20 000 to $120 000. However, this could be a substantial distortion of how much the economy has grown. During the same year prices might also have risen by 20 per cent, so instead of a 20 per cent growth of the economy, it would actually be 0 per cent, because prices increased at the same rate as the change in nominal output.

• Real output is a measure of the value of the real economy in terms of the actual value of goods produced at constant prices. In other words it is not distorted by prices rising. To calculate real GDP using nominal GDP figures it is necessary to adjust for inflation. To do this, use prices in one year and multiply these by the quantity of goods produced.

• For example, if a country only produces one good, mangos, and their price rises from 20 cents to 25 cents between 2010 and 2011, the quantity of mangos produced in the country increases from 100 000 to 110 000 over the same period (see Table 5.4.1).

**Table 5.4.1** Calculating real output

| Production of mangos in 2010 (Q1) | Price per mango in 2010 (P1) | GDP in 2010 (Q1 x P1) |
|---|---|---|
| 100 000 | 20 cents | $20 000 |

| Production of mangos in 2011 (Q2) | Price per mango at 2010 prices (P1) | GDP in 2011 at 2010 prices (Q2 x P1) (real output) |
|---|---|---|
| 110 000 | 20 cents | $22 000 |

Because we have worked with a single set of prices (those for 2010) we are able to calculate the increase in real GDP: from $20 000 in 2010 to $22 000 in 2011.

Calculating the change in nominal income would have given a higher figure as a result of price changes. Nominal income would have risen from $20 000 (P1Q1) to $27 500 (P2Q2) (i.e. 110 000 × 25 cents).

## Output and potential output

Economists are also interested in potential output – that is, the output that could be achieved if all resources were used efficiently. In 1.3 the concept of production possibility curves was introduced.

Potential output takes place at the boundary of the production possibility curve, where all resources are channelled into production. Economies often fall short of their potential output – perhaps because of market failure. Figure 5.4.1 shows the difference between actual output and potential output.

DID YOU KNOW?

Most countries fall short of their potential output because some resources will be unemployed or used inefficiently.

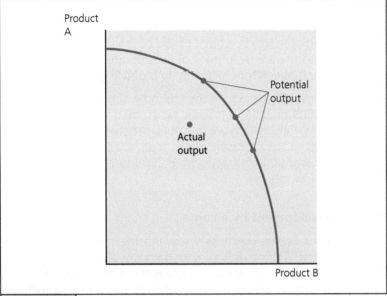

| Figure 5.4.1 | Actual and potential output |

## GDP as a measure of living standards

There are many criticisms of GDP per capita as a measure of the standard of living – that is, how well-off people are in a country. Although it shows the value of goods produced per head of population, it does not give any indication of other important aspects of wellbeing. For example, access to sunshine and a pleasant climate is valuable, but is not considered part of GDP. GDP is also criticised because positive values may be given to goods that some see as harmful, for example military weapons or cigarettes. Measuring GDP per head also fails to take account of inequalities in society. In a country with a very high GDP there may still be people living in extreme poverty. GDP also fails to take account of the negative effects of pollution.

In 5.5 we consider other ways of measuring the standard of living.

KEY POINTS

• Nominal output is the output of an economy expressed in the prices of the day.
• Real output is the output of the economy expressed using constant prices so that comparisons can be made.
• Potential output is the output a country could produce if it used all its resources efficiently.

SUMMARY QUESTION

What is the difference between:

a nominal output and real output

b real output and potential output?

# Economic growth and economic development

Candidates should be able to:

- distinguish between economic growth and economic development
- explain the terms *economic growth, economic development, developing economy, developed economy.*

**Table 5.5.1** Predicted growth of GDP in Barbados

| Year | Barbados $ (billion) |
|------|----------------------|
| 2009 | 1087 |
| 2010 | 1082 |
| 2011 | 1103 |
| 2012 | 1131 |
| 2013 | 1165 |
| 2014 | 1200 |
| 2015 | 1242 |

Barbados ranks as 'very high' in the Human Development Index because of high income per head, long life expectancy and high rates of enrolment in schools coupled with high literacy rates

## Economic growth

Gross domestic product (GDP) measures the total value of goods produced in an economy in a given period of time. Changes in GDP can be used to measure the growth of an economy. Increases in GDP show the increased ability of a country to produce goods.

Table 5.5.1 shows the growth of the economy of Barbados for the period from 2009 to 2015. It is based on estimations of the growth of the economy. Calculations are in Barbados dollars (billions), using prices for 2000 so as to measure real output. You can see from the table that the economy contracted from 2009 to 2010 and then is expected to grow steadily.

## Defining development by income

The World Bank defines countries as low-income, middle-income and high-income. This helps it to make decisions about lending money and supporting development projects in specific countries. Lower-income countries can borrow more finance for development. The World Bank considers low- and middle-income countries to be 'developing'. High-income countries are regarded as 'developed'. Figure 5.5.1 shows a range of countries, from developed to developing.

## Economic development

Disadvantages of measuring the success of an economy only through the growth of GDP include the failure to take several factors into account:

- the harmful effects of producing more goods: for example pollution
- the level of equality in society: most of the GDP might be earned by just a few people rather than being evenly distributed
- the quality of life: people may have more goods, but they are not necessarily better off or happier – GDP does not show whether people live stress-free or healthy lives.

| Low GDP/head<br>Developing | | | | High GDP/head<br>Developed |
|---|---|---|---|---|
| Afghanistan | Zambia | Bangladesh | Algeria | New Zealand | Italy | Singapore |

**Figure 5.5.1** High- and low-income countries

Economic development is a broader measure of improvement in an economy than economic growth. The United Nation's Development Programme has developed the Human Development Index (HDI). The HDI contains three elements:

1 Standard of living as measured by GDP per head

2 Life expectancy at birth

3 Education as measured by:

   a adult literacy (given a weighting of two-thirds)

   b primary, secondary and tertiary enrolment in education (given a weighting of one-third).

Achievement in any of these three areas is measured by how far a country has attained the following goals:

• real GDP per head of US$40 000

• life expectancy of 85 years

• adult literacy and enrolment of 100 per cent.

These goals have not yet been fully attained by any country, so the actual indicators are expressed as decimal shares of the ideal. So 0.5 represents halfway towards the goal. The HDI score for any country is measured between 0 and 1. The highest score is 1.

Using Human Development Indices, countries are ranked into four categories: very high, high, medium and low. Table 5.5.2 shows some of the countries in the very high, medium and low categories, with their ranking in brackets and the HDI score as a decimal.

**Table 5.5.2 Human Development Indicators, 2009**

| Very high | HDI | High | HDI |
|---|---|---|---|
| Norway (1) | 0.971 | Bahrain (39) | 0.895 |
| Australia (2) | 0.970 | Poland (41) | 0.880 |
| New Zealand (3) | 0.950 | Argentina (49) | 0.866 |
| Singapore (23) | 0.944 | Cuba (51) | 0.863 |
| Barbados (37) | 0.903 | Mauritius (81) | 0.804 |

| Medium | HDI | Low | HDI |
|---|---|---|---|
| Thailand (87) | 0.783 | Malawi (160) | 0.493 |
| Iran (88) | 0.782 | Senegal (166) | 0.464 |
| Maldives (95) | 0.773 | Burundi (174) | 0.394 |
| Jamaica (100) | 0.766 | Chad (175) | 0.392 |
| Algeria (104) | 0.754 | Niger (182) | 0.340 |

## Factors influencing economic growth

Several factors affect economic growth. High levels of education and training enable a country's population to engage in complex manufacturing processes and to operate sophisticated service industries. The level of existing physical capital in society is also important, for example the existence of modern communications systems including transport and telecommunications. Access to important natural resources such as natural gas, oil and bauxite help a country to develop and to be less reliant on imported goods and technologies.

KEY POINTS

• Economic growth is an increase in GDP over time.

• Economic development involves increases in GDP coupled with improvements in health, education and other opportunities.

• A developed economy has a relatively high GDP per head and a relatively high HDI.

• A developing country has a relatively low GDP per head and a relatively low HDI.

SUMMARY QUESTIONS

1 If an economy is growing quickly, does this mean that it is developing at the same rate?

2 How can development be measured?

3 What is meant by a developing economy and a developed economy?

# Recession and inflation

Shopping in a supermarket, Trinidad. The Consumer Price Index (CPI) measures general increases in the price of a basket of goods over a period of time. Changes in food prices are particularly important in a country where food is the largest item of household expenditure

## EXAM TIP

Make sure you understand that the price index shows how much the price of an item has risen compared with a base year of 100, while the weighted price index shows the price index times the weight attached to a product category.

## Recession

The economy rarely grows at a steady pace. Sometimes the economy grows relatively quickly, while at other times it grows but only slowly, and occasionally it slips into recession. A recession is a period when for at least two consecutive quarters (3-month periods) the level of GDP falls when compared with the level it was at in the previous quarter.

Figure 5.6.1 shows the recession in Jamaica from 2008 to 2010. You can see that during these years Jamaica had negative growth in its GDP. The recession only officially started after the second quarter of negative growth.

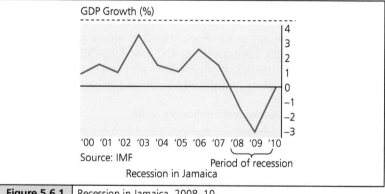

**Figure 5.6.1** | Recession in Jamaica, 2008–10

Recession typically occurs when spending in the economy falls. As a result producers make fewer goods. They employ fewer factors of production. Incomes fall. There is thus a downward cycle of economic activity leading to negative growth in GDP (Figure 5.6.2).

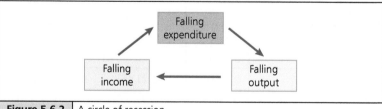

**Figure 5.6.2** | A circle of recession

In the Caribbean, recession is often caused by factors outside the area. For example, a recession in the United States leads to fewer tourists and fewer US imports from the Caribbean. This fall in expenditure triggers a recession in the Caribbean.

## Inflation

Inflation is a persistent or sustained rise in the general level of prices over a period of time. So while not every price will rise, average prices will.

Average prices are measured by governments using the Consumer Price Index (CPI). This measures changes in average prices over a year. Measurements are made by recording prices of goods and services in an imaginary shopping basket – that is, items that most people will be expected to buy. Government statisticians decide what goods to include in the basket. The list should be updated to take account of changing spending patterns.

## Calculating price change

Calculating inflation involves creating a weighted price index. A consumer expenditure survey provides data about typical spending patterns and thus weights. Price changes can then be monitored in a range of retail outlets by trained researchers.

---

**CASE STUDY** | The CPI in Antigua

The starting point is to identify the typical items that an average household in Antigua will buy. Changes in the average price of the basket can then be tracked over time to calculate inflation.

The imaginary shopping basket for a typical family in Antigua contains cereals and bakery products, meat, fruit and vegetables, drinks, clothing and footwear, accommodation rent, fuel and light, and furniture. The contents included in the basket are fixed in the short term, but the prices of individual goods change.

A price index uses a single number to indicate changes in prices of a number of different goods. This is calculated by comparing the price of buying the basket of goods with a starting period, called the base year. The base year is given a figure of 100. So if the average price of goods in the basket today is 10 per cent higher than in the base year, the price index will now be 110. Changes in average prices (the cost of the basket of goods) can be measured on a monthly, quarterly or annual basis. The data for identifying the typical shopping basket for households in Antigua is collected in a Household Income and Expenditure Survey. Data

from 660 households were collected to find out what a typical household purchases. The base year for the index is currently October 2001.

For a period of 2 weeks each month, commencing on the second Tuesday, data are collected to find out the prices of selected items. This makes it possible to calculate changes in average prices since the base year.

Weighting is a figure given to a category of goods according to the percentage of a typical household's income that is spent on it. The total weight attached to all the items in the basket is 1000. The items given the highest weights are food and accommodation, each of which is given a weighting of over 200, because they account for over 20 per cent of the expenditure of a typical Antiguan household.

### Questions

1 Why is such a large weight attached to food in Antigua?

2 If food prices increase substantially, how is this likely to affect the price index?

---

KEY POINTS

- Inflation is a persistent or sustained rise in the general level of prices over time.
- A price index can be used to measure price increases by reducing prices to a single number, starting at 100 in a base year.
- The price index measures change in an average basket of goods bought by a typical consumer or family.

SUMMARY QUESTIONS

1 How is inflation measured?

2 What does *inflation* mean?

3 What is a recession?

4 At what point does a country's economy go into recession?

# Causes and consequences of recession and inflation

Candidates should be able to:

- state the main causes and consequences of recession and inflation in an economy.

Rising oil and energy costs are a major cause of cost-push inflation that affects many businesses across an economy

**DID YOU KNOW?**

Changes in the exchange rate between currencies can have a major impact on business costs. For example, if the Jamaican dollar loses value against the US dollar, people in Jamaica will have to pay more for imported goods from the United States.

## The causes of inflation

Inflation is usually the result of several causes. Economists identify these causes in two sets of factors: cost-push factors and demand-pull factors.

### Cost-push factors

Cost-push factors refer to the costs that a business has to meet, such as wages and raw materials. As costs rise, the business will often pass these on to consumers by increasing the prices for goods they are selling. Major factors are:

- Rises in raw materials costs: in recent years there have been steady increases in the price of oil and gas, as well as of metals and minerals.
- Wage costs: wage rises often follow rises in prices of goods because wage earners, worried that the cost of buying goods is increasing, press for higher wages. Rises in land costs can also cause inflation.
- Imported inflation: Caribbean countries often suffer from this because they import a lot of food and raw materials. Rises in prices of imports will have an impact on costs.

### Demand-pull inflation

Demand-pull inflation occurs when rising demand pushes up the price of goods. This happens when people have more to spend. This is most likely when an economy is near to full employment. Businesses compete for resources and push up prices.

A balance of payments surplus can stimulate demand-pull inflation because this brings more spending power into an economy. When Barbados, for example, runs a balance of payments surplus, people there have more income to spend, helping to push up prices at home. A reduction in taxation by the government can have a similar effect because the government would be taking less money out of the economy, leading to a rise in domestic spending.

Monetary inflation occurs when the quantity of money in the economy rises faster than the quantity of goods. This is described as too much money 'chasing' too few goods. This can happen if the government prints more money or banks increase their lending.

## Consequences of inflation

Table 5.7.1 shows how inflation affects people in different circumstances.

**Table 5.7.1 Effects of inflation on different income groups**

| Income level | Effect of inflation |
|---|---|
| Low income | People can afford fewer goods, including basic necessities; they may resort to buying the lower-priced products available. |
| Fixed income | There is a fall in real income (what can be afforded with money coming in). Because money loses value, people on fixed incomes spend and save less. |
| High income | There is less income to spend on some luxury items. People may therefore switch to cheaper alternatives and cut back on some extravagant purchases. They may save less and spend more. |

**EXAM TIP**

Make it clear in the examination that you understand that inflation can have varying effects on different groups of people in an economy.

Savers and lenders are most likely to lose out in a period of inflation. The value of savings may fall in real terms (savers will be able to buy less with their savings in the future than now). Lenders lose out because they are repaid money that is worth less than it was before the inflation. In contrast, borrowers and people who have bought goods on credit will benefit.

Two additional consequences of inflation are a fall in business confidence and a decline in international competitiveness. Confidence is affected when business people become reluctant to supply goods on credit, because when they come to be paid the value of the money they receive will have fallen. International competitiveness declines when rising prices in the home economy push up the price of exports, making them less attractive to buyers overseas.

## The causes of recession

Recession results from a general fall in spending in the economy. It may be triggered by a fall in spending and trade on a global basis. It may be caused by people saving more and spending less. Recession can also be triggered by a fall in government spending.

### The consequence of recession

A fall in spending leads to a general reduction in output (by firms) and incomes (earned by households), which will have the effect of prolonging recession. Recession leads to a fall in output, incomes and employment. It also leads to a fall in government tax revenues as businesses and households pay less in taxes. Recession can lead to a waste of resources as factories, machines and other productive resources lie idle.

A major consequence of recession for the Caribbean is rising unemployment, with a negative impact on family income. Businesspeople become more pessimistic and less likely to take on new employees.

**KEY POINTS**

- Inflation is caused by demand-pull or cost-push factors.
- Inflation has different effects on different groups.
- Recession is triggered by a general fall in spending.
- Recession results in falling output, income and expenditure.

**SUMMARY QUESTIONS**

1 Explain three common causes of inflation.

2 Explain three common causes of recession.

3 State two consequences of inflation that are harmful to an economy.

4 State two consequences of recession that are harmful to an economy.

# Government management of the economy

Monetary policy involves the control of the quantity of money in circulation and its price (the interest rate)

## Managing the economy

One of the most important roles of the government is that of manager of the national economy. A government minister has overall responsibility for economic policy and he or she will work closely with the central bank and the treasury. The central bank will manage the **monetary policy** and the treasury will manage the **fiscal policy**.

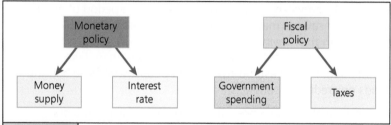

| Figure 5.8.1 | The two main government economic policy instruments |

Monetary policy and fiscal policy are the government's economic instruments for managing the economy. Monetary policy is the control of the quantity (supply) of money and the price of money (interest rate) in order to stabilise the economy. Fiscal policy is the control of the relationship between the level of taxes and government spending in order to stabilise the economy.

The government sends out 'signals' about its monetary policy objectives. One way of doing this is through the 'repo' rate – that is, the discount rate at which it will repurchase government securities. The central bank is the banker for other banks. When they are short of cash they will seek to borrow from the central bank. When private banks are short of cash the central bank will agree to repurchase government securities that banks are holding in order to earn money. When the government lowers the repo rate, this indicates that it is making it easier for banks to borrow and hence lend to its own customers. In contrast, when the government increases the repo rate it is signalling that private banks should lend less because they will have to pay more should they need to borrow from the government.

In a period in which the government considers inflation to be too high it will:

- reduce the money supply
- raise interest rates
- increase taxes
- lower government spending.

In a period in which the government considers that economic growth is too slow or in which there is a recession it will:

- increase the money supply
- lower interest rates
- lower taxes
- increase government spending.

### Fiscal deficit

A fiscal deficit refers to a situation in which the government spends more than it takes out of the economy in taxes. Fiscal deficits are a good way of stimulating the economy. When the government injects more money into the economy through its spending than is taken out in taxes, this will create fresh demand in the economy. Rising demand will encourage businesses to produce more, and to take on more labour. Rising incomes will encourage households to spend more.

### Quantitative easing

In recent years a new expression has entered the vocabulary of economists: **quantitative easing**. This type of monetary policy refers to governments trying to prevent recession by increasing the quantity of money in the economy. To prevent falling expenditures by households and businesses, governments spend, for example on the salaries of public sector workers.

Another monetary policy is to make interest rates low in order to encourage households to spend more and save less, and to encourage businesses to borrow more.

**EXAM TIP**

Make sure that you can explain the difference between monetary and fiscal policy and how they can be used to control inflation and recession.

### KEY POINTS

- Government seeks to stabilise the economy through monetary and fiscal policy.
- Fiscal deficits involve the government spending more than it takes in taxes.
- Reducing interest rates and raising the quantity of money in the economy can be used to stimulate demand.

### SUMMARY QUESTIONS

1 State three approaches that a government can take to reduce inflation.

2 State three approaches that a government can take to help an economy move out of recession.

3 Would the government use the same policies to tackle inflation as it would to tackle recession? Explain your answer.

# Unemployment

## What is unemployment?

Unemployment typically occurs when people who want to work are not able to find jobs. The International Labour Organisation, an agency of the United Nations, defines unemployed people as those who are:

• without a job, but who want a job and have actively sought work in the last 4 weeks and are available to start work in the next 2 weeks

• out of work, have found a job and are waiting to start it in the next 2 weeks.

## What causes unemployment?

Unemployment is caused by a range of factors, some of which are more harmful than others in that they affect more people and have a longer-term impact on the economy. Figure 5.9.1 shows the range of unemployment types: the factors that cause them are explained in the next paragraphs.

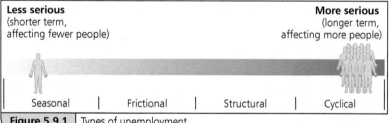

| Less serious (shorter term, affecting fewer people) | | | More serious (longer term, affecting more people) |
| --- | --- | --- | --- |
| Seasonal | Frictional | Structural | Cyclical |

**Figure 5.9.1** | Types of unemployment

• **Seasonal unemployment** occurs where there are distinct seasons, for example the tourist season or the sugar cane harvest season. For part of the year, for example at harvest time, there will be plenty of jobs. In the rainy season, fewer jobs will be available.

• **Frictional unemployment** occurs when the market system does not work as smoothly as it should. This sort of unemployment occurs where there is a mismatch between the demand for and the supply of labour. This might occur when employees are trying to recruit highly skilled construction workers but too few workers have been trained with the skills required. It may also be temporary unemployment, occurring while people are leaving one job to go to another.

• **Structural unemployment** arises when there are longer-term changes in the economy affecting specific industries, regions and occupations. For example, the move from farming to manufacturing and then on to services has led to rural and urban poverty in areas where agriculture and manufacturing are in decline. It may also occur when new technologies enable labour savings to be made, but workers become unemployed as a result.

- **Cyclical unemployment** is on a larger scale and relates to periods of economic growth and periods of recession. Cyclical unemployment is unemployment that occurs during a recession. It can last for the best part of a year, or much longer if the recession is prolonged.

### Real wage unemployment

If trade unions push up wages above the market rate, this can cause unemployment. Where people are being paid a higher money wage than what the market would pay them for their work, businesses may lay off some labour.

Some economists believe that unemployment is also caused when the government sets minimum wages at higher than the market rate. You can see from Figure 5.9.2 how this would happen. The market labour rate would be at the point where demand for labour cuts the supply of labour. However, if the government sets a minimum wage above this level, there will be many more people looking for work at this level than the demand for labour at the minimum wage (see the level of unemployment in the diagram).

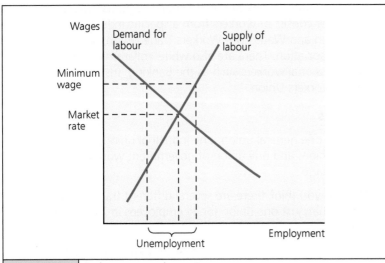

**Figure 5.9.2** | Real wage unemployment

### Measures to reduce unemployment

Government approaches to reducing unemployment need to be related to its type. Governments are unlikely to be concerned about seasonal unemployment, though they may try to create government work schemes in certain seasons.

Solutions to frictional unemployment include government training schemes and more information about job availability. Structural unemployment can be tackled through government subsidies to encourage growth of new industries. Cyclical unemployment needs to be tackled through the monetary and fiscal policies explained in 5.8.

**SUMMARY QUESTIONS**

1 Explain the main differences between:

  a structural and cyclical unemployment

  b frictional and seasonal unemployment.

2 What approaches could a government take to tackle structural unemployment?

3 How might these approaches be different to the ones that it would use to tackle cyclical unemployment?

# Trade unions in the economy

Taxis in Trinidad: the Taxi Drivers Association is an example of a union consisting of workers from a specific industry.

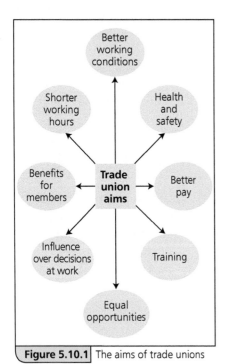

**Figure 5.10.1** The aims of trade unions

## What is a trade union?

A **trade union** is an association of employees formed to protect and promote the interests of its members. Trade unions are formed, financed and run by their members, who pay an annual subscription. The unions try to influence some of the decisions made by the owners and managers of businesses. Public sector unions bargain with government-appointed public sector employers.

| CASE STUDY | Trade unions in Trinidad and Tobago |
| --- | --- |

Trinidad and Tobago has more trade unions than any other Caribbean territory. It has trade unions representing employees who work for the government, such as the National Union of Government Employees, and the Trade Union Congress. These unions will negotiate directly with the government. The National Trades Union Council is a union of workers from many different industries. Some unions can be described as industrial unions in that they consist of workers from a specific industry, such as the Seamen and Waterfront Workers Trade Union, and the Taxi Drivers Association. There are also white-collar unions, of office and professional workers,such as the Banking, Insurance and General Workers Union.

**Questions**

1 Identify one general union, one industrial union, one white-collar union, and one union of government workers in Trinidad and Tobago.

2 Why do you think there are several different trade unions rather than just one union for all employees in Trinidad and Tobago?

3 Why do you think there are so many different unions in Trinidad and Tobago?

Figure 5.10.1 shows some of the aims of trade unions. You can see that the main aim is to secure the best possible conditions of work for members. Unions know that the decisions a firm makes will affect the livelihoods of workers and their families.

## The effect of trade union action

The benefit of trade union action is that it helps to raise the wages, conditions and esteem of unionised labour. This is likely to result in greater motivation and better employee health, in turn making labour more productive and efficient.

The drawback of trade union action is that wages may rise above the market clearing level, and labour becomes more expensive as a result, which may lead to substitution by other factors of production such as automatic machinery – in other words, unemployment. Union action may also increase inflation. This type of inflation is described as wage-push inflation – because wages are a major cost of production of most goods.

## Negotiation

One of the purposes of a trade union is to negotiate – that is, discuss with employers. Talks take place between the representatives of the employees (union officials) and representatives of the employer. Both sides try to reach agreement on issues such as conditions of employment (e.g. hours worked, safety of the workplace) or wage levels. This negotiation takes place at a local level (e.g. within a factory) or at national level, where the union represents all the members of the trade union in the country.

Figure 5.10.2 illustrates the bargaining range.

## Trade union membership: the benefit to individuals

Typical benefits of belonging to a trade union include:

- knowing that you are part of a group that represents you and fellow workers
- belonging to a body that negotiates better terms and conditions (e.g. pay increase, improved conditions) for you
- direct benefits (e.g. sickness benefit)
- support for members if there is a grievance (e.g. if a member of a trade union feels they have been treated badly at work) or disciplinary procedure (e.g. when a union member has been disciplined, perhaps for poor timekeeping)
- direct action to support members (e.g. if negotiations over pay break down with employees, union officials may call a strike; this means that union members stop work).

The ability to strike gives unions considerable power: if airline or railway workers go on strike, their companies lose money, profit and their reputation for reliability. Other actions that unions can take include working more slowly (a go-slow) and working to rule – only doing things that fit strictly with the rules set out in a contract of employment.

## Trade unions: the impact on the economy

Trade unions may play an important part in determining wages. Where unions are strong they have power to push up wages, increasing costs. In some countries workers' representatives are part of company decision-making. In Germany elected works councils make suggestions about the running of the business. In contrast, unions may call frequent strikes, which can lead to unemployment and disruption.

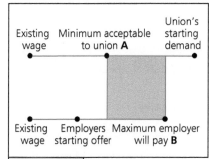

**Figure 5.10.2** The bargaining range: this falls between point A and point B

### KEY POINTS

1 Trade unions are set up to protect the interests of their members.

2 Trade unions negotiate with employers and try to secure better working conditions.

3 Trade unions protect the interests of workers within the wider economy. Their leaders meet regularly with government officials and employer representatives.

### SUMMARY QUESTIONS

1 What are the main purposes of trade unions?

2 How do trade unions interact with employers' organisations to determine wages and conditions?

# Section 5    Practice exam questions

## SECTION 1: Multiple-choice questions

1 The main components of the circular flow of income are:

   a   Banks and customers

   b   Households and firms

   c   Workers and trade unions

   d   The public sector and government

2 Net property income from abroad is used to distinguish between:

   a   Gross domestic product and capital consumption

   b   Gross domestic product and national income

   c   Gross domestic product and gross national product

   d   Gross domestic product and taxes and subsidies

3 The value of gross investment will be higher than the figure for net investment because of the effect of:

   a   Taxes

   b   Subsidies

   c   Capital consumption

   d   Net property income

4 A type of inflation is:

   a   Demand-pull

   b   Demand-push

   c   Deflation

   d   Depreciation

5 A government can relieve a recession by:

   a   Selling government bonds

   b   Buying government bonds

   c   Operating a budget surplus

   d   Increasing direct taxation

6 The price index in a given year is 115 and the nominal GDP is $8000. What is the real GDP rounded to the nearest whole number?

   a   6957

   b   6900

   c   7885

   d   920 000

7 GDP represents:

   a   Local production by nationals of the country only

   b   Production by nationals of a country residing in other countries

   c   Local production by nationals and foreigners residing in the country

   d   Local production by foreigners only residing in the country

8 The main type of unemployment found in the tourism industry is:

   a   Structural

   b   Frictional

   c   Real wage

   d   Seasonal

9 A fiscal deficit occurs when:

   a   Government expenditure is greater than government revenue

   b   Government expenditure is less than government revenue

   c   Subsidies are greater than taxes

   d   Taxes are greater than subsidies

10 Withdrawals from the circular flow of income comprise:

   a   Savings + taxes + consumption

   b   Government spending + imports + investment

   c   Exports + taxes + government expenditure

   d   Savings + taxes + imports

1 a  Define the term *national debt*. (*2 marks*)

 b  List three withdrawals from the circular flow of income. (*3 marks*)

 c  Explain two benefits a worker can gain from being a member of a trade union. (*6 marks*)

 d  Analyse two problems that can arise from using GNP to measure the standard of living. (*4 marks*)

2 a  Define *monetary policy*. (*2 marks*)

 b  List three injections into the circular flow of income. (*3 marks*)

 c  Explain two ways in which the government can increase employment in the economy. (*6 marks*)

 d  Using a numerical example, differentiate between nominal and real output. (*4 marks*)

3 a  State the meaning of the following terms:

  i  GDP

  ii  GNP. (*2 marks*)

 b  List three main injections into the circular flow of income. (*3 marks*)

 c  Differentiate between nominal, real and potential output. (*6 marks*)

 d  Compare two differences between GDP and GNP, in developed countries versus developing countries. (*4 marks*)

4 a  Define the terms:

  i  unemployment

  ii  disposable income. (*4 marks*)

 b  List three types of unemployment. (*3 marks*)

 c  Explain how the expenditure approach is used to calculate GDP. (*8 marks*)

 d  Explain how trade unions may contribute to unemployment by bargaining for higher wages. (*5 marks*)

5 a  Define inflation. (*2 marks*)

 b  Identify two types of business costs that might arise and hence raise the level of inflation in a Caribbean economy. (*2 marks*)

 c  List three consequences of inflation. (*3 marks*)

 d  Explain two ways in which fiscal policy can be used to reduce inflation in the economy. (*8 marks*)

 e  Explain two ways in which natural disasters can affect economic growth. (*5 marks*)

# Why countries trade

Guyana has a comparative advantage in the production of sugar

## Comparative advantage

Countries and regions concentrate on producing the things that they are best at rather than wasting resources on products that they make less efficiently. Economists explain this in terms of the **law of comparative advantage**. This sets out that a country will specialise on the lines in which it has the greatest relative advantage.

## The gains from trade

International trade takes place between two or more countries. The benefits to a country are:

• being able to sell to a wider market (exporting)

• being able to buy a wider range of goods and services (importing)

• being able to buy better goods than those produced domestically

• being able to concentrate on the most efficient lines

• developing cooperative and political links with other countries.

## Why do countries trade?

Consider the following case. Once there were two islands separated by a sea that was too dangerous to cross. On the first island, which was very flat, grain could be grown in plenty, but the waters around the island contained few fish. The second island was very rocky and only a little grain could be grown. However, around this second island, fish were plentiful.

One day an explorer found a sea passage enabling trade to take place between the islands.

Before the trade route was discovered, half of the people in each island spent their time farming, and the other half spent their time fishing.

Table 6.1.1 shows the amount of grain and fish that could be produced in a year.

Table 6.1.1 Output of two islands before specialisation occurs

|  | Grain production (baskets) | Fish production (baskets) |
|---|---|---|
| Rocky Island | 20 | 100 |
| Flat Island | 100 | 20 |
| Total | 120 | 120 |

## Comparative advantage and gains from trade

Comparative advantage results from one country having a lower opportunity cost than other countries in the production of the goods in which it specialises.

Because of the islands' natural differences, Rocky Island is comparatively more efficient at producing fish, while Flat Island is comparatively more efficient at producing corn. What is the effect of opening up the trading route? Assuming that the islanders are happy to cooperate, each island could concentrate on the product in which it has a comparative advantage. Rocky Island focuses on fish and Flat Island focuses on corn. Table 6.1.2 shows the resulting position.

**Table 6.1.2  Output of two islands after specialisation**

|  | Grain production (baskets) | Fish production (baskets) |
|---|---|---|
| Rocky Island | 0 | 200 |
| Flat Island | 200 | 0 |
| Total | 200 | 200 |

Total production of the two products will increase from 120 baskets of each (before specialisation) to 200 of each (after specialisation). The two countries can now trade. People on Rocky Island will be better off, provided that they can exchange 1 basket of fish for at least 1/5th of a basket of corn. People on Flat Island will be better off, provided that they can exchange one basket of corn for at least 1/5th of a basket of fish. (This is because without trade in Rocky Island, for each basket of fish produced, 1/5th of a basket of grain would have to be given up. Without trade in Flat Island for each basket of grain produced, 1/5th of a basket of fish would have to be given up.)

The parties to trade all benefit. Countries importing goods are able to do this for less than it would cost to produce them in the domestic market. Countries exporting are able to sell goods abroad on better terms than they would receive in their domestic market.

## Specialisation in Caribbean economies

The law of comparative advantage goes some way to explaining specialisation in Caribbean economies, although government protection of some industries is also an important reason. Some specialisation is based on historical patterns of production. Antigua and Barbuda specialise in agriculture, rum, cotton goods and light assembly goods. Dominica focuses on ecotourism, soap and coconut oil. Jamaica focuses on recorded music, bauxite, mining, coffee, spices, hot peppers, cocoa and bananas. See if you can find out the specialisms of other Caribbean countries. How important is the law of comparative advantage in explaining these specialisms?

# Factors that influence the level of trade

Candidates should be able to:

- describe factors that influence the level of international trade.

Other countries import oil from Trinidad because they are not able to produce oil on an economic scale themselves

## Absolute and comparative advantage

For many years Trinidad was famous for growing sugar cane. It can no longer produce sugar on the huge scale and low cost of countries like Brazil and India. Today Trinidad imports sugar, while Brazil is perhaps the world's most efficient and largest sugar producer. Brazil thus has an absolute advantage relative to countries like Trinidad in producing sugar. It also has a **comparative advantage** in the production of sugar because it has a lower opportunity cost than Trinidad.

A country has an absolute advantage over its trading partners if it is able to produce more of a good or service with the same amount of resources, or if it can produce the same amount with fewer resources. A country has a comparative advantage in producing a good at a lower opportunity cost than a trading partner.

So today Trinidad concentrates on other lines, such as natural gas production in which it has a comparative advantage. Trinidad now benefits from concentrating resources on natural gas rather than sugar.

## Factors that influence the level of trade

### Importing

Caribbean economies import many goods from other parts of the Caribbean, North and South America and further afield. Why do they need to import so much?

- To obtain products that cannot be produced naturally in the domestic economy: for example, other parts of the Caribbean import oil from Trinidad because they do not have their own oilfields.
- To obtain products that can be produced more cheaply elsewhere: comparative advantage is a factor. Most islands in the Caribbean can grow bananas using available land. However, it makes more sense to import bananas from the Windward Islands, which is an efficient grower. The opportunity cost of growing bananas in other parts of the Caribbean may be too high: the land can be used more efficiently for other purposes.
- Importing gives consumers a greater choice of goods.
- Importing also provides greater competition in the domestic market, encouraging more efficient production.

| CASE STUDY | Rare earths |
|---|---|

Rare earths are precious minerals used in high-tech electronics, magnets and other products. Until recently over 90 per cent of the world's supplies were found in China. Rare earths are an important component of flat-screen television sets and hybrid cars. This meant that countries producing these goods, such as Japan, had to import rare earths from China, and the price was rising steadily. However, in 2011 Japanese scientists discovered large deposits of rare earths on the bed of the Pacific Ocean and they are hoping to exploit these reserves in the near future for commercial purposes.

### Questions

1 Why do countries like Japan need to import rare earths?

2 What products can you think of that your country has to import because:

**a** the product is not found or produced in the domestic economy

**b** the opportunity cost of making the product domestically would be too great?

## Exporting

The leading exports within CARICOM (a group of Caribbean economies that trade freely with each other – see Section 7) are oil from Trinidad and bauxite and alumina from Jamaica. Tourism is also a major export for many Caribbean economies.

Trinidad is the Caribbean's leading exporting economy, largely as a result of the benefits resulting from its oil industry. The oil industry provides Trinidad with a relatively cheap source of fuel, enabling comparatively cheap production of other industrial products such as asphalt, ammonia and iron.

The level of exports of Caribbean economies depends on the following:

• The availability of resources in that country: Trinidad, Jamaica and Barbados, for example, have, on balance, greater quantities of natural resources than other island economies.

• The level of development of those resources: Trinidad has developed a number of manufacturing industries, enabling it to manufacture and export.

• The ability to exploit **economies of scale**, the cost advantages that result from producing on a larger scale: many Caribbean economies are at a disadvantage through their relatively small size and the resulting small-scale production. However, where mass production approaches are employed, costs can be reduced. An example is tourism provision, with some small territories now having quite extensive airport, hotel and leisure facilities.

• The need to export: Caribbean countries have always been exporting nations, partly because of the need to earn foreign exchange in order to import essential items such as food and fuel.

# Terms of trade

Candidates should be able to:

• explain the concept of *terms of trade*.

## What are the terms of trade?

**Terms of trade** is a measure of the quantity of imports that can be purchased through selling a fixed quantity of exports. If the number of imports that can be obtained for a set quantity of exports increases, the terms of trade improve. If the number of imports that can be obtained for a set quantity of exports decreases, the terms of trade deteriorate. The terms of trade can be measured by the formula:

Terms of trade = Price of exports/Price of imports

The prices index is calculated by creating an index of export prices and import prices. The index starts from a base year in which the index is set at 100.

**Table 6.3.1 Improving terms of trade**

| Example 1 | Index of export prices | Index of import prices |
|---|---|---|
| Year 1 (base year) | 100 | 100 |
| Year 2 | 120 | 100 |

Table 6.3.1 shows that the terms of trade have improved because the country can now purchase a greater quantity of imports for the same quantity of exports. This is because the price of exports has increased by 20 per cent while the price of imports has remained the same.

**Table 6.3.2 Deteriorating terms of trade**

| Example 2 | Index of export prices | Index of import prices |
|---|---|---|
| Year 1 (base year) | 100 | 100 |
| Year 5 | 120 | 150 |

Table 6.3.2 shows that the terms of trade have deteriorated over time because the country can now only purchase a smaller quantity of imports for the same quantity of exports. This is because the price of exports has increased by 20 per cent while the price of imports has risen by 50 per cent.

**DID YOU KNOW?**

An index number is a figure reflecting a change in value or quantity as compared with a standard or base. The base usually equals 100 and the index number is usually expressed in terms of that base. The terms of trade index focuses on relative changes in export prices compared with import prices.

**EXAM TIP**

You should be able to explain that the terms of trade index is particularly significant in a Caribbean context. Countries that have traditionally focused on exporting agricultural commodities have often suffered as the index of agricultural prices has fallen relative to the price of manufactured imports.

**CASE STUDY** | Island and Mainland

The terms of trade can be illustrated by a situation in which there are only two countries and they trade only two products. We will call these two countries 'Island' and 'Mainland'. If Island exchanges $50 worth of goods for $100 worth of goods from Mainland, then its terms of trade are 50:100 – that is, 0.5.

If this is the case then Mainland's terms of trade with Island are 100:50 — that is, 2.0.

From the point of view of Island, if the terms of trade fall, say from 0.5 to 0.4, then the terms of trade will be deteriorating, because Island is having to trade more of its own products to receive the same value of imports.

## Questions

1 If the price of Island's exports rises faster than the price of its imports, what is happening to its terms of trade with Mainland? Explain your answer.

2 In what circumstances might Island's terms of trade with Mainland improve?

**DID YOU KNOW?**

The terms of trade (TOT) is influenced by the exchange rate because a rise in the value of a country's currency lowers the price of imports. A fall in the value of a country's currency raises the price of imports.

## Elasticity of demand

Elasticity of demand for exports is a measure of the responsiveness of the demand for exports to a general increase or decrease in their prices.

$$\text{Export elasticity of demand} = \frac{\text{\% change in quantity of exports demanded}}{\text{\% change in export prices}}$$

A similar formula can be used to measure the elasticity of demand for imports (to do this you would simply replace the term 'exports' with that of 'imports').

It is important to be cautious about the benefits of improvements in the terms of trade. When the price of exports of your country rises relative to the price of imports, the terms of trade are said to have improved. However, this does not tell the full story in terms of whether your country gains from this change. If the demand for your exports is relatively elastic, your country may sell many fewer exports as a result of an improvement in the terms of trade. If the demand for imports in your country is relatively inelastic, then your citizens may spend a lot more money on imports as a result of a rise in the price of imports. So it is important to consider not only the terms of trade but also the elasticity of demand for exports and imports.

**SUMMARY QUESTIONS**

1 Set out the formula for the terms of trade.

2 Explain whether the following would lead to an improvement or a deterioration in the terms of trade for Jamaica:

   a  the price of the country's exports rising while the price of its imports fall

   b  the price of its imports rising faster than the price of exports

   c  the price of its exports rising while the price of its imports remains the same.

**KEY POINTS**

• Terms of trade measures the price of exports compared with the price of imports.

• Terms of trade improve when more imports can be purchased with a given quantity of exports.

• Improvements in terms of trade do not necessarily benefit a country.

# Exchange rates

When a country imports tractors it will usually have to pay for those tractors in the currency of the country it is importing from, for example from the United States in US dollars

## EXAM TIP

*Make sure you can show an understanding of both the causes and the consequences of exchange rate fluctuations.*

## The exchange rate

When you buy sea island cotton T-shirts or other items of clothing produced in Barbados you will want to pay for them in the currency of your own country (unless of course you live in Barbados). The T-shirts are likely to have been imported into your country by a specialist importer or a large retailer. The T-shirt manufacturer in Barbados will not want to be paid by the importer in the currency of your country. This is because the manufacturer will need to pay its own workers and suppliers of cotton in Barbados dollars. The importer will therefore need to purchase Barbados dollars to pay the manufacturer in Barbados. Foreign currency can be bought and sold in the foreign exchange market (or FOREX). This market specialises in exchanging Barbados dollars, Eastern Caribbean dollars, yuan, rupees and other currencies.

The exchange rate between two currencies is determined by demand and supply. If the demand for US dollars by Indians (to buy American goods) rises quickly, while the demand for rupees by Americans (to buy Indian goods) remains steady, then the value of the dollar will rise against the rupee, for example from US\$1 = 45 rupees to US\$1 = 47 rupees.

You can see from this analysis that a major determinant of the value of a currency is how popular the currency is – that is, the strength of demand for it. One of the major factors influencing demand is the extent to which foreigners want to buy goods from that country. For example, the Singapore dollar tends to be a relatively strong currency because many foreigners buy goods from Singaporean companies.

Another factor strengthening a currency is its use for international trading. For example, the US dollar has for many years been used by countries for trading because it tends to keep its value over time.

## Reasons for changes in exchange rates

The following will lead to a rise in the value of a country's currency against other currencies:

• an increase in the interest rate in the country (relative to that in other countries), leading to a flow of investment into the country attracted by the higher interest rate

• a balance of payments surplus, which will help to raise the exchange rate as foreigners are demanding more of the country's currency to pay for goods.

The value of the currency in international exchange will fall as a result of a balance of payments deficit, and/or a fall in the interest rate compared with interest rates in other countries.

## Multiple exchange rates

There is not just one exchange rate for a currency: it can often be exchanged for the currencies of many other countries, for example the Jamaican dollar against the Eastern Caribbean dollar, the Jamaican dollar against the US dollar, the Jamaican dollar against the euro, and so on.

## Exchange rate systems

A government may decide to use fixed or floating exchange rates:

- **Fixed exchange rates**: the value of the currency is fixed against another currency or group of currencies. For example, the rate of exchange is fixed at US$1 = Barbados $2. This fixed rate is maintained by the government. For example, the government could set the exchange rate such that two dollars of your currency may be exchanged for one US dollar. This helps to make the currency stable. However, it may make it difficult for the country to sell its goods on international markets if the exchange rate is set at too high a level for exporters to be competitive. A disadvantage of having a fixed rate is that the government has to support the existing rate even when the rate makes it difficult for exporters to sell their goods competitively.

- **Floating exchange rates**: the value of your currency changes from day to day according to the demand and supply for it. If we are finding it difficult to sell exports the currency will fall in price (as demand falls). Lowering the price of exports makes them more competitive – and hopefully sales will improve.

| CASE STUDY | Exchange rates for the Eastern Caribbean dollar |
|---|---|

On 7 July 2011 the Eastern Caribbean Central Bank published the following list of exchange rates of its dollar against other currencies:

| | |
|---|---|
| Pound sterling £ | 4.31 |
| Canadian $ | 2.80 |
| Euro € | 3.86 |
| US$ | 2.68 |
| Barbados $ | 1.35 |
| Guyana $ | 0.01 |

You can see that the rate of exchange of the Eastern Caribbean dollar to other currencies varies considerably. There are multiple exchange rates.

### Questions

1 How many pounds sterling could have been obtained for 100 Eastern Caribbean dollars?

2 How many Eastern Caribbean dollars could have been exchanged for 100 euros?

**SUMMARY QUESTIONS**

1 What is an exchange rate?

2 How is an exchange rate determined?

# Types of exchange rate

The exchange rate between the US dollar and the Barbados dollar is fixed at Barbados $2 = US$1

## Exchange rate regimes

**Exchange rate regime** refers to the way in which a country's exchange rate is determined. Figure 6.5.1 shows how the exchange rate regime in a country falls along a spectrum.

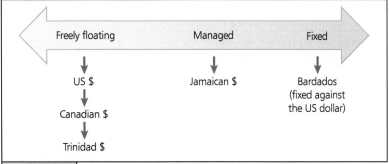

| **Figure 6.5.1** | Different types of exchange rate regimes |

## Fixed exchange rate

A fixed rate is the rate at which a central bank sets and maintains an official exchange rate, for example Barbados $2 = US$1. The rate of exchange of the local currency (Barbados dollar) is fixed against a major world currency. This helps to provide stability for the Barbados dollar in Barbados and gives users confidence because they know that in Barbados they can exchange their dollars for an internationally recognised exchange currency (the US dollar).

Advantages of having a fixed rate are:

- It helps to create a stable environment for foreign investment. Investors know that the value of the Barbados dollar is stable.
- A fixed rate usually leads to lower inflation rates because the price of imports remains stable.

A disadvantage of having a fixed rate is:

- If the rate is fixed at too high a level it may be difficult to maintain. This can lead to a financial crisis because the home currency is overvalued, making it difficult to export goods. Investors and speculators may rush to sell the overvalued currency, forcing the central bank to revalue it at a lower level.

## Floating rates

A floating rate is one that is determined on a day-to-day basis by demand and supply in the market. If demand for a currency is low its value will fall, making imported goods more expensive and encouraging demand for locally produced goods. The demand from foreigners for exports will increase. Floating exchange rates are described as being 'self-correcting'. Increased demand for the currency raises its price. Falling demand for the currency lowers its price.

Advantages of floating rates are:

- They lead to 'self-correcting' in the economy. The exchange rate changes day by day so that a sudden economic crisis does not arise, as in the case of a fixed rate.
- The exchange rate is determined by the market. There is no outside interference by the central bank.

Disadvantages of floating exchange rates are:

- Investors cannot be certain about the return on their investment because the value of the currency of the country they are investing in changes on a day-to-day basis.
- Falls in the value of the currency can lead to 'imported inflation' as the price of imports increases.

Guyana, Suriname, and Trinidad and Tobago operate with floating exchange rates.

## Managed rates

A managed exchange rate is a combination of fixed and floating exchange rates. The central bank allows the exchange rate to fluctuate between an upper and a lower rate. For example, in 2011 the Jamaican dollar was allowed by the Central Bank of Jamaica to fluctuate between limits of 40 and 44 Jamaican dollars to the Barbados dollar.

The advantage of managed floating is:

- The exchange rate is more flexible than a fixed rate, but more stable than a freely floating rate.

A disadvantage is:

- The exchange rate is not as stable as a purely fixed rate, and not as flexible as a freely floating exchange rate.

## SUMMARY QUESTIONS

1 What is an exchange rate regime?

2 What are the three main types of exchange rate regime?

3 Identify Caribbean countries that have fixed exchange rates. Against what are they fixed?

4 Distinguish between each of:
   a   currency appreciation and depreciation
   b   currency revaluation and devaluation.

# Causes of exchange rate fluctuations

The US dollar is used widely as a generally acceptable international exchange currency

## Appreciation and depreciation

Another way of looking at the exchange rate is as the price of buying the currency of one country with that of another country. Like other prices, the exchange rate will then be determined by the demand for and supply of it.

If more people in India want to buy US dollars, the demand curve will shift to the right and the price of dollars will increase when bought with rupees. This may be because more Indians want to import goods from the US. Figure 6.6.1 shows this change. It is referred to as an **appreciation** in the price of the dollar. (In contrast, if Indians want to buy fewer goods from the US, this leads to a fall in demand for dollars and a fall in value – that is, **depreciation** – of the dollar.)

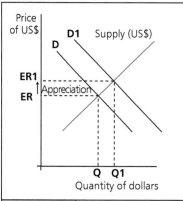

| **Figure 6.6.1** | An appreciation of the dollar against the rupee |

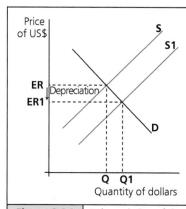

| **Figure 6.6.2** | A depreciation of the dollar against the euro |

The price of a currency may fall as a result of an increase in the supply of that currency, for example as a result of citizens of that country using their domestic currency to buy more imports. An example of this is that the US dollar is accepted widely as an international trading currency and more and more dollars have been entering the international exchange market. The increase in supply of dollars over time (see Figure 6.6.2) leads to its depreciation against other currencies, such as the European Union's euro. For the last 20 years the US has been running large current account deficits with the rest of the world. This has helped the world economy because US dollars are widely accepted as a means of international exchange.

Under a system of freely floating exchange rates the value of currencies will appreciate and depreciate continually, in line with changes in demand for and supply of currencies for international exchange.

Foreign exchange is bought and sold for trading purposes and also for investment, such as buying shares in companies in other countries. Some people also buy currency in order to speculate, for example to buy at a low price and sell when prices rise.

## Devaluation and revaluation

**Revaluation** of a currency occurs when its value is adjusted. For example, the rate of exchange between a country's currency and the US dollar was previously 10 units to one US dollar. Now the government changes the rate to 5 units equal to one US dollar. This would make the dollars half as expensive to people wanting to buy them with the revalued currency.

In a system where exchange rates are fixed against other currencies, they may become overvalued over time. For example, a country might find that at the existing exchange rate it is difficult for exporters to compete with cheaper (or better-quality) products from rival countries. The government may then have to act and devalue the currency – that is, force the exchange rate down. The central bank would be instructed to supply an increased quantity of the currency onto international markets. This would reduce its price and bring about **devaluation** (see Figure 6.6.3), and at the same time make imports more expensive. These two effects would help to improve the current account balance.

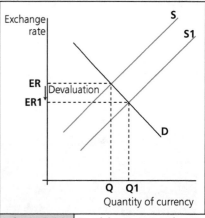

**Figure 6.6.3** Devaluing a currency by increasing its supply

### KEY POINTS

1 Fluctuations in exchange rates are caused by changes in the supply and demand of international currencies.

2 Changes in demand and supply for currencies result from the demand and supply of currencies for trade purposes, and for capital flows.

3 Speculation can lead to unsettling changes in the price of foreign exchange.

### EXAM TIP

Make sure that you understand the difference between an appreciation and a revaluation, and a depreciation and a devaluation of a currency.

### SUMMARY QUESTIONS

1 How might a change in the demand for East Caribbean dollars (by consumers in the United States buying more goods from East Caribbean countries) lead to a change in the exchange rate of the Eastern Caribbean dollar against the US dollar?

2 Explain the difference between each of:
   a  depreciation and devaluation
   b  appreciation and revaluation.

# The balance of payments and the balance of trade

Bananas are the top visible export of the Windward Islands

## The balance of trade

The **balance of trade** in goods and services accounts shows the flows of money coming into and going out of a country as a result of trading. Balance of trade also refers to the net figure after imports have been deducted from exports.

The balance of trade account shows transactions relating to two types of items:

- visibles – trade in physical goods
- invisibles – trade in services.

### Trade in visibles (physical goods)

**Visible trade** involves items that you can actually see, physical goods that a country trades. For example, Trinidad's top export is oil, while the top export from the Windward Islands is bananas.

So for Guyana, visible exports are goods sold by Guyanese citizens to other countries. They bring revenue into the country. Over 75 per cent of Guyana's visible exports consist of sugar, bauxite, rice and gold.

Visible imports are purchases by Guyanese citizens of goods from other countries. Guyana's main visible imports are machinery, petroleum and food.

### Trade in services (invisible items)

**Invisible trade** involves non-physical trade items. For many Caribbean countries, major invisible exports are tourism and financial services.

So for Barbados, invisible exports are services sold by its citizens to other countries. The main invisible exports of tourism and financial services bring revenue into Barbados.

An example of an invisible import – that is, a service bought by a citizen of Barbados from another country – might be the owners of a hotel in Barbados insuring their hotel with a foreign insurance company.

## The balance of trade account

Table 6.7.1 shows Jamaica's balance of trade in 2008. The first part shows the goods (visible balance). The second part shows the services (invisible balance). The third part shows the balance of trade. You can see that Jamaica had a deficit on its balance of trade (mainly as a result of importing more goods than it sold).

**Table 6.7.1** Balance of trade for Jamaica, February 2008 (US$ millions)

| 1 Goods balance | −264.9 |
|---|---|
| Exports | +231.6 |
| Imports | −496.5 |
| 2 Services balance | +49.0 |
| Transportation | −41.8 |
| Travel | +135.5 |
| Other services | −44.7 |
| 3 Balance of trade | −215.9 |

**EXAM TIP**

You should be able to calculate the value of the balance of trade from a list of entries setting out the values of different types of exports and imports.

## The balance of payments

The **balance of trade account** is very useful in presenting a picture of the relationship between current exports and imports in a country. The term should not be confused with the 'balance of payments', which provides a much wider picture of all the flows of money coming into and leaving a country in a particular period of time.

For example, we saw in Table 6.7.1 that Jamaica ran a balance of trade deficit in 2008 of $215.9 million. The balance of payments provides details of how this deficit was financed. As a financial statement the balance of payments will always balance because it shows that:

• if there is a deficit on the trade account how this deficit is paid for
• if there is a surplus on the trade account what happens to this surplus.

## Current account and capital account

In 6.8 we shall see how the balance of payments consists of both a current account and a capital account. The current account consists of the balance of trade and some other receipts and payments that a country pays or receives during a given year or other time period. The capital account sets out totals of borrowing and sales of assets that a country makes in a period of time. The easiest way to think of the capital account is as an account showing totals related to investment activities.

**KEY POINTS**

• The balance of trade shows payments and receipts from imports and exports.
• The balance of payments shows all payments and receipts involving a country in a given period of time.
• The current account of the balance of payments sets out payments and receipts involving transfers of money for current activities.
• The capital account is concerned with flows of funds for investment activity.

**SUMMARY QUESTIONS**

1 What is the difference between the current account and the capital account?

2 What is the difference between the balance of payments and the balance of trade?

# Constituent components of the balance of payments

## The balance of payments

The balance of payments (BoP) is an account measuring transactions between one country and the rest of the world in a given time period.

---

**CASE STUDY** | Balance of payments, Barbados, 2009

Table 6.8.1 shows the main components of the balance of payments account for Barbados in 2009.

**Table 6.8.1** Barbados's BoP, 2009

|  | Barbados $ million |
|---|---|
| 1 Visible trade 1(a) − 1(b) | −1825.6 |
| 1(a) Exports | 762.1 |
| 1(b) Imports | 2587.7 |
| 2 Services (net) | 1441.3 |
| 3 Income (net) | −158.7 |
| 4 Current transfers (net) | 57.6 |
| 5 Current balance (1+2+3+4) | −485.4 |
| 6 Capital and financial account | 643.8 |
| 7 Errors and omissions | −80.4 |
| 8 Balance for official financing (5+6+7) | 78.1 |
| 9 Change in reserves | −78.1 |

Items 1–4 make up the current account. You can see that on the visible trade balance Barbados imported a greater value of goods than it exported. The services balance showed a substantial inflow of net revenue for Barbados. The income section consists of two elements: income received from citizens of Barbados who are working abroad and sending money home, and income in the form of profits and dividends earned by Barbados citizens from their investments abroad. Current transfers are moneys that flow into Barbados in the form of gifts, such as presents to Barbados citizens from relatives abroad and aid from other governments to the Barbados government.

The current account balance therefore consists of (1+2+3+4).

The sixth item that appears in the balance of payments is for the capital account and financial account. The capital account includes funds brought into Barbados by new immigrants, and funds sent abroad by people emigrating from Barbados. It also includes international transfers of funds for the purchase (and sale) of fixed assets. The financial account records the movement of funds for the purchase of companies and shares in companies. When citizens of Barbados buy assets abroad this appears as a negative figure; when foreigners buy assets in Barbados this counts as a positive figure. You can see that on the capital and financial account there was a substantial inflow of funds to Barbados.

In calculating the figures in the balance of payments account some mistakes (errors) are made and some items are left out by mistake (omissions). Those responsible for creating the balance of payments account therefore need to include an item for errors and omissions.

When government statisticians calculate (5+6+7) they are in a position to see how much is needed to balance the accounts. This is referred to as the balance for official financing. In 2009, the figure was Barbados $78.1 million.

In 2009 this was balanced off by an increase in the currency reserves held by the Central Bank of Barbados.

**Questions**

1 Why do you think that Barbados had a visible trade deficit in 2009?

2 Why do you think that the income figure was negative?

3 Why do you think that the current transfers figure was positive?

## Key items in the balance of payments account

The Barbados example shows the way that the balance of payments is broken up into the following sections:

1 Visible trade: exports (+) and imports (−) of goods. Typically Caribbean economies have a negative visible balance because they rely on imported food and manufactured goods.

2 Invisible trade: exports (+) and imports (−) of services. Many Caribbean economies have a positive visible balance as a result of tourism.

3 Income: 1. Including wages and salaries earned by a country's nationals working abroad; 2. Profits and dividends earned by overseas operations of a country's companies.

4 Current transfers: gifts, charitable donations and flows of aid.

5 The current balance consists of 1+2+3+4.

6 The capital and financial account. The capital account consists of funds brought into the country by new immigrants (or leaving the country with emigrants). The financial account shows investment into (and leaving) a country.

7 Errors (mistakes) and omissions (items left out) when making records.

8 The balance for official financing: this is the figure that is left after making the calculation 5+6+7.

9 Balancing the account: if the balance for official financing is a positive figure, this will be balanced by an increase in the reserves of foreign currency held by the central bank (this is shown as a negative figure in the change in reserves). If the balance for official financing is a negative figure, this will be balanced by a reduction in the reserves of foreign currencies held by the central bank (this is shown as a positive figure in the change in reserves). The account can also be balanced by borrowing money internationally, for example from the International Monetary Fund, when official financing is required to balance the account. When a country runs a surplus, it can repay some of these loans.

# 6.9

# Balance of payments surplus

China is the country with the largest balance of payments surplus. Manufactured goods like textiles provide an important component of this surplus

## DID YOU KNOW?

The term *Dutch disease* was used to describe a situation where a country exports a lot of natural resources (natural gas in the case of Holland). The high level of exports of natural resources leads to a rise in the value of the currency as foreigners seek to buy it. The consequence is to make the exports of other goods and services increasingly difficult because of the rising price of the currency.

## Balance of payments surplus

A balance of payments surplus occurs when the payments made by a country are less than the payments it receives: more currency flows into the country than flows out.

This can occur when:

1 The country is running a balance of payment surplus on its current account. In recent years the Chinese economy has consistently made more exports than imports of goods and services. Some people refer to this economy as the 'world's factory', producing large quantities of manufactured goods that are sold across the globe. The Chinese government has been able to use this surplus on the current account to invest in a range of projects worldwide. It has purchased companies producing minerals and metals in a number of countries.

2 The country is running a balance of payments surplus on its current account and capital and financial accounts combined. The overall effect of this is a net inflow of funds to a country. This net inflow can be used either to:

- pay off international borrowing from previous years
- build up reserves of foreign currencies.

## Causes of payments surplus

Reasons for a country having a balance of payments surplus include the following:

- The country is very efficient at producing goods and services that other countries want. Germany is very effective at producing high-quality engineering products and cars.
- The country has several natural resources that it is able to sell on world markets. Middle Eastern countries are able to export a lot of oil.
- The country is able to attract considerable foreign capital investment. This might be because of opportunities for investment there, or because the country offers a higher rate of interest.

Having a balance of payments surplus is not always a good thing, as is outlined in the next paragraph.

## The consequences of running a surplus

The main consequence of running a surplus is a rise in the value of the currency of that country. On the foreign exchange market (FOREX) there will be an increased level of demand for its currency in order to buy its goods and invest there. Another consequence on the international scale is that if one country has a surplus, one or more other countries will have a deficit, potentially leading to problems for countries that are persistently in deficit, as the value of their currencies fall.

The reserves of foreign currency in the surplus country will increase. It will also be able to pay off some or all of its loans to lenders such as the International Monetary Fund (IMF).

Running a surplus on the current account provides a country with more capital which it can then reinvest overseas. In recent years China has invested billions of dollars in projects in the Caribbean, including the construction of roads, hotel and leisure complexes, and cricket stadiums. Once a country has invested through capital and financial flows, it can expect to benefit from income (profits and dividends) in the current account.

Countries that run balance of payments surpluses find that the extra money flowing into their domestic economy leads to rising prosperity and wage increases, resulting in higher levels of inflation.

## Remedies for surpluses

A balance of payments surplus is seen as less serious than a balance of payments deficit (see 6.10). Large countries, such as China, building up huge surpluses can cause problems for the world economy, unless the country reinvests the surplus. Running surpluses can only be achieved if other countries run deficits. So a surplus country must be careful because other countries will not be able to run deficits forever. If a surplus country allows the value of its currency to rise, its goods and services will become more expensive and less attractive to buyers. A key remedy for a surplus therefore is for the surplus country to allow its currency to appreciate, to reduce or eliminate the surplus. Another way to cut back surpluses is to eliminate protection for any domestic industries so that they are exposed to international competition.

**EXAM TIP**

Make sure that you can explain the difference between a trade surplus and a trade deficit and how they might arise. Surpluses may appear in the current account, the capital account or a combination of these two accounts.

**KEY POINTS**

- A trade surplus exists when a country receives more revenue than it pays out in a given period.
- Trade surpluses arise when a country has an efficient economy.
- A trade surplus usually leads to a rise in the exchange rate of a country's currency.

**SUMMARY QUESTIONS**

1 How might a country come to have a balance of payments surplus?

2 What will be the impact on reserves if that surplus is maintained over a period of years?

**DID YOU KNOW?**

A balance of payments deficit builds up problems for the future. For example a large current account deficit can usually only be financed through borrowing (and/or running down reserves). Borrowing needs to be repaid by a country in the future, plus interest charges. The deficit can also lead to a loss in value of the currency in terms of its exchange rate.

**EXAM TIP**

Make sure you can explain both the causes of deficits (e.g. importing more goods from overseas than the value of exports) and the consequences of deficits (e.g. having to borrow and run down reserves).

## Balance of payments deficits

A balance of payments deficit occurs when a country has a negative current account balance, usually because it imports more than it exports. A balance of payments deficit will also occur if the combined value of inflows on the current account and capital financial account is less than the outflows on these accounts.

Balance of payments deficits can lead to a serious drain on a country's resources in order to pay for the deficit. For example the Statistical Institute of Jamaica (a government body) reported that Jamaica's total expenditure on imports in the period January to August 2011 was valued at US$4323.9 million, compared with earnings from total exports of US$1113.0 million. The deficit had become increasingly severe in the period leading up to 2011 because of the increasing cost of fuel and food imports, particularly from the United States (which accounts for one-third of all imports).

Building up a payments deficit becomes increasingly problematic because a country (in this case, Jamaica) would need to borrow in order to finance the deficit. The more a country borrows, the more it will have to pay back and the higher the interest rate to lenders will become.

## Factors leading to a deficit and their consequences

A country will run a deficit when payments made to other countries are greater than payments received. A major reason for this will be a lack of competitiveness of its exports on world markets. Until the 1990s Caribbean economies were traditional exporters of a range of agricultural products, including sugar and bananas. In the face of large-scale plantation agriculture, however, particularly in Latin America, these agricultural exports have become less competitive. Natural causes can also affect these exports: hurricanes can lead to a sharp fall in output, and in 2009 and 2010 the banana exports of Grenada and Dominica fell by almost 20 per cent as a result of an infestation of black sigatoka leaf spot disease. Tourism has been a major export earner for many parts of the Caribbean, but revenues have been insufficient to cover rising import costs.

The consequences of a current account deficit are that:

- a country has to borrow or run down its reserves to pay for a deficit
- borrowing is unsustainable in the long period – lenders will impose higher and higher interest rates and may eventually refuse to lend
- the export sector may be good at creating jobs, for example in hotels and leisure facilities, but a decline in the export sector leads to a loss of jobs
- a balance of payments deficit can lead to a loss of confidence in

the country's currency, leading in turn to a fall in its exchange rate against other currencies.

> **DID YOU KNOW?**
>
> Barbados always keeps a minimum of 3 months' worth of foreign exchange in its reserves to make sure that it can cover trade deficits that could lead to a loss of confidence in the Barbados dollar.

## Remedies for balance of payments deficits

Remedies that can be applied to deal with deficits include the following:

• Restricting imports: a quota is imposed, limiting the number of imports in a given period. An import tariff, a tax, can be imposed on the number of imports (for example $1 per item) or on the value of goods (for example $1 tax for every $10 of imports). Imports can also be restricted by limiting the amount of foreign currency that citizens can hold.

• Encouraging exports with a subsidy (reverse tax): the government could also subsidise new and growing industries that are likely to lead to future exports.

• Encouraging an inflow of capital: raising interest rates is one way of encouraging foreigners to invest in a country. The government can also make it easy for foreign partners to invest in a country.

• A fall in the value of a country's currency: this will also help to increase exports, as goods from that country become cheaper. Imports also become more expensive.

> **DID YOU KNOW?**
>
> CET stands for common external tariff. For example when a group of countries like CARICOM establishes a customs union, they will set out a common external tariff. This is a tariff set at the same rate and imposed on imports from countries outside the customs union.

The best way for a country to reduce balance of payments deficits is to become more competitive by developing efficient industries. A good way to do this is to invest in modern education and training.

Different remedies for deficits will have different impacts. Restricting imports and subsidising exports may be criticised because they are protective measures and go against the principles of free trade which the World Trade Organisation is seeking to encourage. In contrast, allowing the currency to depreciate will make exports more competitive without interfering with principles of the free market.

> **KEY POINTS**
>
> • A balance of payments deficit arises when payments made by a country are greater than receipts.
>
> • A deficit often arises through a country's industries failing to be competitive in international markets.
>
> • The government can intervene to reduce deficits by taxing imports and subsidising exports.

> **SUMMARY QUESTIONS**
>
> 1 What is a balance of payments deficit?
>
> 2 How can a sustained run of deficits over a period of years lead to problems for an economy?
>
> 3 How would that economy balance its balance of payments account?

# Section 6    Practice exam questions

SECTION 1: Multiple-choice questions

1 A devaluation of a currency occurs under:

   a  A floating exchange rate

   b  A managed exchange rate

   c  A fixed exchange rate

   d  An adjustable peg exchange rate

2 Three types of protectionist measure are:

   a  Tariffs, quotas and exports

   b  Tariffs, quotas and imports

   c  Tariffs, exports and imports

   d  Tariffs, quotas and administrative barriers

3 A deficit on the balance of trade shows that:

   a  Imports are greater than exports

   b  Exports are greater than imports

   c  Government spending is greater than taxes

   d  Taxes are less than government spending

4 Which of the following can *most likely* improve a deficit on the balance of payments?

   a  A revaluation of the currency

   b  A devaluation of the currency

   c  An increase in government spending

   d  A decrease in interest rates to stimulate credit availability

5 Which of the following items are found in the current account?

   a  Exports, imports and short-term loans

   b  Exports, imports and direct investment

   c  Short-term loans, direct investment and foreign reserves

   d  Exports, imports and investment income

6 CET is the abbreviated form for:

   a  Caribbean external trade

   b  Common external tariff

   c  Caribbean export transactions

   d  Caribbean environmental treaty

7 Investment income represents:

   a  Interest, profits and dividends

   b  Foreign direct investment

   c  The purchase of local shares by foreign businesses

   d  Short-term capital loans

8 The WTO is:

   a  A negotiating body to settle trade disputes

   b  A development bank that lends for long-term projects

   c  A stock exchange to monitor the sale and purchase of securities

   d  A world bank that lends money when countries are in difficulty

9 A balance of payments:

   a  Never balances

   b  Always balances

   c  Sums to a negative number

   d  Sums to a positive number

10 The comparative advantage theory states that:

   a  A country should export the good in which it has a lower opportunity cost of production

   b  A country should export the good in which it has a higher opportunity cost of production

   c  A country should import the good in which it has a lower opportunity cost of production

   d  A country should import the good if climatic conditions are unfavourable

1 a  State what the following represent:
    i CET  ii WTO. (*2 marks*)

  b  List three reasons why countries trade.
    (*3 marks*)

  c  Explain three consequences of a balance of
    payments deficit to a country. (*6 marks*)

  d  Analyse the impact that a serious
    earthquake in Haiti will have on two
    items in the balance of payments of that
    country. (*4 marks*)

2 a  Define the terms: i quota ii tariff. (*4 marks*)

  b  List one reason why countries protect their
    markets. (*1 mark*)

  c  Explain three ways in which a country can
    seek to improve a balance of payments
    deficit. (*6 marks*)

  d  Barbados under a fixed exchange rate
    system has decided to adjust its currency
    rate from US$1 = Barbados $2 to US$1 =
    Barbados $4. Explain what has happened
    to the Barbadian exchange rate. (*4 marks*)

3 a  Define the terms: i fixed exchange
    ii devaluation. (*4 marks*)

  b  State one factor that influences the
    exchange rate of a country. (*1 mark*)

  c  Explain three factors that give rise to a
    balance of payments deficit. (*6 marks*)

  d  Differentiate between a tariff and a
    common external tariff. (*4 marks*)

4 a  Define the terms: i balance of trade
    ii balance of payments. (*4 marks*)

  b  List three types of exchange rate regimes.
    (*3 marks*)

  c  Describe two factors that would cause an
    appreciation of a currency. (*8 marks*)

  d  Explain how devaluation affects a
    country's balance of trade. (*5 marks*)

5 a  Define the terms: i comparative advantage
    ii absolute advantage. (*4 marks*)

  b  List three items other than the balance of
    trade that would be found in the balance
    of payments of a country. (*3 marks*)

  c  Explain the production and consumption
    gains from trade according to the
    comparative principle. (*8 marks*)

  d  The table below shows a country's trading
    patterns. Calculate the current account
    balance of the country's balance of
    payments. (*5 marks*)

|  | $ billions |
|---|---|
| Exports of goods | 25 000 |
| Exports of services | 50 000 |
| Imports of goods | 30 000 |
| Imports of services | 15 000 |
| Transfers | 20 000 |
| Net investment income | −10 000 |

# 7 Caribbean economies in a global environment

## 7.1

# Characteristics of Caribbean economies

With a population of only 39 000, St Kitts and Nevis has little opportunity for economies of scale

## Size of Caribbean economies

One of the major challenges facing Caribbean economies in a globalised economy is that they are relatively small. Table 7.1.1 shows approximate population sizes for selected territories.

**Table 7.1.1** Approximate population for selected Caribbean territories, 2011

| Territory | Population |
|---|---|
| Cuba | 11.5 million |
| Jamaica | 2.8 million |
| Trinidad and Tobago | 1.4 million |
| Guyana | 800 000 |
| Barbados | 300 000 |
| St Lucia | 170 000 |
| St Vincent and the Grenadines | 110 000 |
| St Kitts and Nevis | 39 000 |
| Anguilla | 15 000 |

The number of people available to produce and consume goods in these countries is thus relatively small when compared with larger territories (Table 7.1.2).

**Table 7.1.2** Approximate population for selected large territories, 2011

| Country | Population |
|---|---|
| Germany | 82 million |
| United States | 306 million |
| China | 1.3 billion |

Not only do Caribbean economies have relatively small populations, but their relatively small land areas give access to fewer natural resources. A problem of being a small economy is that the opportunity to exploit economies of scale is limited. One of the basic principles of economics is that the ability of a country or region to specialise is determined by the size of the market. The larger the market, the more specialisation that can take place.

## Natural resources

The Caribbean has access to plentiful resources in the form of sunshine, sea and attractive landscapes. These resources give the Caribbean the greatest comparative advantage with different types of tourism: premium-class holidays and ecotourism in more remote areas that are rich in natural habitats. Another advantage of these resources is that foreigners obviously have to come to the Caribbean to enjoy them. The 'goods' do not have to be transported overseas. Other natural resources are specific to particular parts of the Caribbean, such as oil in Trinidad and bauxite in Guyana. Most Caribbean islands are effective producers of agricultural products: bananas, sugar, peppers, pineapples. However, agriculture tends to be relatively inefficient on a global scale when compared with the huge plantations in Latin and South America.

## Terms of trade

The Caribbean region was traditionally an agricultural producer. Many of the products, such as cane sugar and bananas, were traded in European markets where they were allowed open access with no import tariffs. However, agricultural products are 'low-value-added products': they sell for relatively low prices because there is a lot of competition from sugar and bananas produced in other parts of the world. Caribbean economies were therefore exporting low-value-added goods. However, they were importing high-value-added goods, for example cars and radios, which are produced using complex processes and are heavily branded, advertised and marketed. Caribbean economies were thus exchanging relatively low-priced goods for relatively high-priced goods – resulting in poor terms of trade.

The terms of trade of an economy or region can be calculated using the following formula (using Jamaica as an example):

$$\text{Jamaica's terms of trade} = \frac{\text{Jamaica's average export price index}}{\text{Jamaica's average import price index}} \times \frac{100}{1}$$

Terms of trade improve in the following scenarios:

- export prices rise faster than import prices
- export prices fall less than import prices
- export prices rise with import prices the same
- export prices stay the same and import prices fall.

## Dependency

Another feature of Caribbean economies is dependency. This is looked at in more detail in 7.2. Dependency results from relying on other countries. For example, tourism to the Caribbean depends substantially on tourists from North America and Europe. Periods of recession in those economies affect the Caribbean. Another source of dependency stems from borrowing from overseas to finance balance of payments deficits. Repayments on loans mean that substantial parts of the national income of Caribbean economies is spent on servicing – that is, repaying – debt.

### DID YOU KNOW?

Other aspects of the dependency of Caribbean economies include:

- vulnerability to natural disasters such as hurricanes
- heavy dependence on trade agreements, for example with the United States and the European Union
- small market size because of low populations.

### KEY POINTS

- Caribbean economies are small and have limited land areas.
- However, they are rich in resources such as sunshine, access to the sea and its products, and unspoilt landscapes.
- Dependency on international markets is an issue for Caribbean economies.

### SUMMARY QUESTIONS

1 What is the difference between the size of Caribbean economies and those of competing economies such as the United States, Canada, Brazil and Venezuela?

2 What natural advantages do Caribbean economies have?

# Problems for Caribbean economies

Candidates should be able to:

- state the major problems associated with Caribbean economies.

Barbados has vibrant music and arts industries, including top artist Rihanna

**DID YOU KNOW?**

Relatively small economies can reach global markets by focusing on being competitive in the supply of products such as IT, music and film that have global appeal.

## Limited export base

A major problem for Caribbean economies has been their traditional reliance on one or a small number of exports. For example, St Lucia has a traditional reliance on the export of bananas to the UK, and in the 1960s the economy of Barbados was heavily dependent on sugar exports.

In the 1960s St Lucia was able to export over 80 per cent of the bananas it produced to the UK. The problem of depending on a narrow export base is that when that base is damaged, the whole economy suffers. In 2007 St Lucia was badly hit by Hurricane Dean, with a devastating impact on export earnings.

The agricultural sectors of Caribbean economies used to have preferential trading relations with the UK, with many agricultural products allowed to enter the UK free of import taxes. At the same time rival exporters were required by the UK to pay often quite substantial tariffs. After the UK became a member of the European Union, these conditions were altered, to the detriment of many Caribbean economies. In some areas of St Lucia where there was a heavy dependency on banana growing, there are now high levels of unemployment. In recent years, however, St Lucia has diversified its economy around new areas of growth, such as information technology and tourism.

| CASE STUDY | Diversifying the economy in Barbados |
| --- | --- |

Barbados provides a good example of a country that has diversified its economy in order to counteract the problems of dependency and reliance on a narrow range of exports.

Sugar cane was the major export in the 1960s, but the situation is reversed today, with much less sugar being produced for export. Instead Barbados has focused on a range of modern products and services.

The prime export is tourism. The strong tourism industry has encouraged the development of a range of other industries such as construction, and the products associated with tourism, for example beach towels and sun-protection products. More significantly there has been a diversification into other modern industries including fashion design and fashion labels. The music industry is also important, including the development of Ice recording studios and international artists such as Rihanna. The government of Barbados is also encouraging the development of film studios on the island. Barbados is well known for having some of the best education facilities in the world, including a major campus of the University of the West Indies. The health sector is another growth area, with the development of specialist high-quality hospitals with an international reputation.

The government of Barbados also encourages the development of small businesses, by providing management training courses and business advice centres. Barbados also has some outstanding sports and leisure facilities, including an internationally renowned test cricket ground and a racecourse. Information technology and offshore banking industries are also important in Barbados.

This example shows how being a small island economy can actually be an advantage, but education is a key driver in creating an enterprising and capable workforce able to compete on an international scale.

### Questions

**1** How has Barbados been able to counteract some of the problems associated with relatively small island economies?

**2** Is it possible to extend the Barbados model of a dynamic island economy across the Caribbean?

## Brain drain

A key problem faced by Caribbean economies has been a 'brain drain', coupled with a 'skills drain'. The Caribbean area is internationally renowned for its high-quality education system. There were, however, insufficient jobs for well-trained and educated employees. As a result many highly qualified young people emigrated to the United States and Europe. In addition, countries with skills shortages actively recruited nurses, teachers, police officers and skilled workers from the Caribbean area. The Caribbean was thus effectively spending large sums on training people for the benefit of other countries. The brain drain is likely to continue because relatively small countries cannot create the number of professional and skilled jobs required to meet the ambitions of young and talented people. However, diversification of the economy in the way outlined in the case study provides a model for retaining people within the home economy. A diversified economy provides many different opportunities.

### DID YOU KNOW?

One of the Barbados government's ambitious schemes is to create a 'brain train', with the objective of having at least one university graduate in every home in Barbados.

### KEY POINTS

- Problems for Caribbean economies include dependency on one or a small number of exports, exposure to natural disasters, and a brain drain of skilled and professional workers.

- These problems can be combated by diversifying the economy.

### SUMMARY QUESTIONS

1 State what you consider to be the five most serious problems facing many Caribbean economies.

2 What is a 'brain drain'? How is a brain drain likely to have an adverse effect on the efficiency of a Caribbean economy?

# More about Caribbean economies

## Debt burden

Many Caribbean economies have a high debt burden, which has its origins in borrowing by previous national governments. Debts are built up when countries invest in infrastructure such as airports, roads and bridges. Debts may be owed to international bodies such as the International Monetary Fund (IMF), overseas governments and private investors.

The current high-level debt burden of Grenada is equivalent to 110 per cent of its GDP. The higher the debt burden, the higher the rate of interest an economy will have to pay on loans, and the greater the proportion of current resources that have to be used to service the debt. Grenada was particularly badly hit by Hurricane Ivan in 2004 and Hurricane Emily in 2005. The impact of Emily was estimated to be the equivalent of 2 years' GDP for the island.

The debt burden of an economy can be measured by calculating the national debt as a percentage of GDP:

$$\text{Debt burden} = \frac{\text{National debt}}{\text{GDP}} \times \frac{100}{1}$$

IMF figures in 2010 showed that St Kitts and Nevis had a debt burden of 196 per cent, while the figure for Trinidad was much lower, nearer to 40 per cent. The national debt is the total debt of the national government.

## Structural adjustment

Lending bodies such as the IMF or the World Bank will only lend on the condition that a country restructures its economy. **Structural adjustments** are conditions for receiving new loans or for obtaining lower interest rates on existing loans. Borrowers may be expected to implement free market policies such as privatising state industries and reducing government regulation of business activity. Countries are also expected to reduce trade barriers such as import taxes. A criticism of World Bank and IMF structural adjustment programmes is that the policies and plans are often framed by planners working for these organisations rather than by the countries receiving the loans. Structural adjustment plans have often required Caribbean countries to cut back on public sector spending, social services and jobs.

Hurricane Emily had a devastating effect on Grenada, requiring a lot of borrowing to restructure the economy

## Economic integration

A key move in the Caribbean in recent years has been towards economic integration. This involves measures such as allowing free movement of people, goods and capital within the CARICOM area. Taxes on the export and import of goods are removed for most goods. Parts of the Caribbean area, for example the Eastern Caribbean Currency Union, are also integrated through having a common currency. Various stages of economic integration are covered in 7.4.

### KEY POINTS

- Debt burdens arise from past borrowing. They represent loans that need to be repaid with interest.
- Structural adjustment programmes are wide-scale changes that need to be made by an economy in return for loans from the IMF and World Bank.
- Increasingly Caribbean economies are setting out their own plans for structural adjustment.

### SUMMARY QUESTIONS

1 How might having a large debt burden result in an economy being asked to make structural adjustments?

2 What are the implications for the independence or dependency of an economy?

# CARICOM

## Protectionism and laissez-faire

A protectionist and a *laissez-faire* set of economic relations between countries lie at opposite ends of the spectrum (Figure 7.4.1).

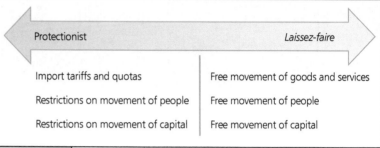

| Protectionist | Laissez-faire |
|---|---|
| Import tariffs and quotas | Free movement of goods and services |
| Restrictions on movement of people | Free movement of people |
| Restrictions on movement of capital | Free movement of capital |

**Figure 7.4.1** Economic relations between countries

Protectionism involves protecting a country's domestic economy and producers against foreign competition through measures such as imposing taxes on imports and physical limitations on the number of imports (quotas). *Laissez-faire,* in contrast, means non-interference in trading and other economic arrangements, allowing the three freedoms of movement: of goods and services, labour and capital.

## Different levels of economic integration

Figure 7.4.2 shows different levels of economic integration between countries.

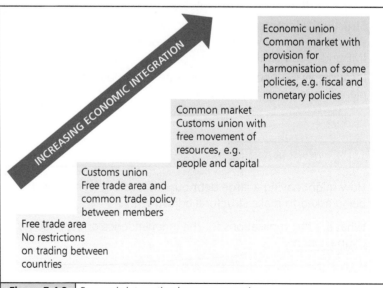

INCREASING ECONOMIC INTEGRATION

Economic union
Common market with provision for harmonisation of some policies, e.g. fiscal and monetary policies

Common market
Customs union with free movement of resources, e.g. people and capital

Customs union
Free trade area and common trade policy between members

Free trade area
No restrictions on trading between countries

**Figure 7.4.2** Economic integration between countries

# CARICOM

CARICOM is the Caribbean Community. It is an organisation of 15 Caribbean economies (plus some additional states with associate member status) that seek to enable the three freedoms outlined above. CARICOM originally came into being in 1973 as the Caribbean Community and Common Market, when it consisted only of Barbados, Jamaica, Guyana, and Trinidad and Tobago. The original intention of the Community was to enable the free movement of goods and services between the four founder members. It was set up by the Treaty of Chaguaramas.

The current full members of CARICOM are Antigua and Barbuda, Bahamas (not part of customs union), Barbados, Belize, Dominica, Grenada, Guyana, Haiti (although subject to free and fair elections), Jamaica, Montserrat, St Kitts and Nevis, St Lucia, St Vincent and the Grenadines, Suriname, and Trinidad and Tobago.

Important features of CARICOM are:

- free movement of goods and services
- the right of establishment: that is, for CARICOM-owned businesses to set up in other member states without restrictions
- a common external tariff: that is, agreed common import taxes for products from non-member states
- free movement of capital from one country to another and convertibility of one currency into another
- a common trade policy
- free movement of labour
- harmonisation of a number of business laws such as those relating to intellectual property rights.

The role of Chair (Head) of CARICOM is rotated among the heads of state of the member economies. Committees of Ministers of CARICOM seek to work together to harmonise policies of the member states, for example in relation to development. CARICOM consists of 20 different institutions, including the Caribbean Examinations Council, the Caribbean Disaster Emergency Response Agency and the Caribbean Competition Commission.

## CARICOM and the EU

The level of integration of CARICOM can be compared with that of the European Union (Table 7.4.1).

**Table 7.4.1** Levels of integration in CARICOM and the EU

|  | Free trade area | Customs union | Common market | Economic union |
|---|---|---|---|---|
| EU | ✓ | ✓ | ✓ | ✓ |
| CARICOM | ✓ | ✓ | ✓ | Working towards a fuller economic union |

# Modern trading arrangements

Globalisation enables products to be transported from one part of the globe to another

## Globalisation

**Globalisation** refers to the convergence of lifestyles and products across the globe. Large quantities of products can be transported across the globe on huge freight-carrying ships. Globalisation presents both a challenge and an opportunity for the Caribbean. The biggest challenge is that mass-produced products can be distributed to the Caribbean from much larger countries (such as China and Brazil) at a very low cost. Some people are concerned at the disappearance of regional distinctions. The opportunities provided are for Caribbean countries to export products to a global market. Instant communications through internet links mean that, for example, producers of niche products such as recording, film and art studios can now export to the globe through internet-based sales outlets. The development of air links has made the Caribbean region one of the prime global destinations for tourism.

## Trade liberalisation

Over the last 20 years the World Trade Organisation (WTO) has played a major role worldwide in liberalising, or freeing up, trade. The WTO, with its headquarters in Geneva, Switzerland, became a permanent organisation in 1995. It encourages and supervises agreements between member countries to reduce tariffs, quotas and other trade restrictions and encourage moves away from protectionism. Trade liberalisation enables countries to focus on lines in which they have the greatest comparative advantage. As a result world trade increases, leading to higher levels of global production and the lowering of prices of goods.

Today, member nations of the WTO represent over 97 per cent of the world's population. Since China joined in 2001 there has been a progressive fall in the price of many manufactured goods and textiles that China produces on a large scale. While this is a good thing for consumers who can now buy cheaper textiles, it is bad for manufacturers and employees in countries – including Caribbean nations – trying to sell textiles onto regional and international markets.

## Bilateral and multilateral agreements

A *bi*lateral trade agreement is between two individual countries, while a *multi*lateral agreement is the result of negotiations between several countries at the same time.

A good example of a bilateral agreement is the PetroCaribe agreement between Venezuela and individual Caribbean states in 2005 and beyond. The agreement was for Venezuela to supply oil to Caribbean countries in exchange for part-payments within 90 days, followed by repayments over a period of 23–25 years, with a 1 per cent rate of interest. In this case some Caribbean countries welcomed the opportunity, while others rejected it: Trinidad and Tobago was already the main supplier of oil to the Caribbean, and Barbados too turned downed the opportunity because it did not want to become indebted to Venezuela.

Multilateral agreements are between at least three, and often many more, countries. In 1975 the Lomé Convention was signed between what is now the European Union and former colonies, known as the African, Caribbean and Pacific (ACP) group. Part of this agreement concerned a system whereby there would be no tariffs in the EU on many goods, mainly agricultural, entering from ACP countries.

The Banana Protocol was a multilateral agreement that no ACP state would suffer from the development of the European Union. The protocol became a source of dispute between the EU and many other countries, particularly Latin American countries and the United States, trying to export bananas to the EU.

## The WTO and multilateral agreements

In recent years the WTO has played a major role in helping countries to develop multilateral agreements to lower tariff barriers and quotas on a global scale. The belief is that the expansion of global trade will benefit the growth of economies across the world, helping to create new jobs and providing development opportunities.

### KEY POINTS

- Globalisation involves increased movement of goods in international markets and growing similarities in lifestyles.
- Trade liberalisation has led to a rapid expansion of world trade.
- Bilateral agreements are trading arrangements involving two countries, whereas multilateral ones involve three or more countries.

### SUMMARY QUESTIONS

1 Define globalisation in your own words.

2 How does trade liberalisation contribute to globalisation?

3 What is the difference between a bilateral and a multilateral trade agreement?

# The IMF and the World Bank

Candidates should be able to:

- explain the purpose and function of the IMF and the World Bank.

The International Monetary Fund exists to help countries with balance of payments deficits and other financial problems

**DID YOU KNOW?**

Before the Second World War there had been increasing protectionism and restrictions on trade between countries. What was needed afterwards were international financial systems that would create more confidence and lead to an increase in world trade.

**DID YOU KNOW?**

Today, the World Bank focuses on poverty reduction in less developed countries and encourages clean technology projects that combat air and water pollution.

## Setting up the IMF and the World Bank

The World Bank and the IMF were set up in 1944 around the end of the Second World War, in an attempt to reconstruct the world economy. Their headquarters are in Washington DC. These organisations are agencies of the United Nations.

## The World Bank

The World Bank originally set out to lend money to governments seeking to rebuild their economies after the Second World War. Its first loan was of $250 million, to France. There were conditions attached, for example making sure that the country ran a balanced (rather than a deficit) budget. Increasingly the emphasis of World Bank projects shifted to lending to developing countries.

Table 7.6.1 summarises the focus of loans since the establishment of the World Bank.

**Table 7.6.1** World Bank loans

| Period | Type of project |
|---|---|
| Up to 1968 | Projects that would lead to repayments in the medium to long term: to build dams, roads, ports and other transport links |
| 1968 to 1980 | Emphasis switched to projects designed to meet the basic needs of people in the developing world, e.g. building schools and hospitals |
| During the 1980s | Emphasis switched again to structural adjustment programmes, e.g. privatisation of government-owned industries and encouraging competition between businesses – this approach was criticised for interfering too much in the economies of developing countries |
| Since the 1990s | More emphasis on encouraging national governments, aid agencies and environmental groups to be more active in setting World Bank lending priorities |

## The IMF

While the focus of the World Bank is on big capital projects and training, the IMF focuses more on short-term issues and balance of payments problems.

- The IMF's objective is to encourage global growth and economic stability.

In March 2011 The World Bank approved a US$15 million zero-interest credit to St Lucia to repair hurricane damage to the island's infrastructure and improve long-term ability to withstand disasters.

As a result of Hurricane Tomas on 30 October 2010, river banks were washed away and bridges, homes and parts of roads were destroyed. The hurricane led to flash flooding and landslides. The impact of the damage was most severe for the vulnerable, that is low-income households, but agriculture and tourism were also severely affected

The World Bank loan included provision for the reconstruction of damaged schools, hospitals, community centres and roads. New hurricane-resistant building standards were established. In addition, funding was provided for government ministries and the National Emergency Management Organisation to assess risks and develop appropriate plans to limit these in the future.

### Questions

1 What was the objective of the World Bank in providing credit to St Lucia?

2 What evidence is there that the finance focused on long-term projects?

- It provides policy advice to member countries with financial difficulties.
- The International Monetary Fund encourages monetary cooperation and seeks to create exchange rate stability.
- It provides financial support for countries with balance of payments difficulties.
- The IMF works with developing countries to create economic stability and to reduce poverty.
- It monitors the economies of its 187 member countries, raising awareness of likely future risks.

In 2010 the IMF agreed to provide the Jamaican government with a credit for US$1.27 billion on account of the country's high balance of payments deficit and fiscal deficit. Like many other countries, Jamaica was suffering from the global economic recession in 2008–09, with substantial foreign debts tied to high-interest payments.

The IMF made the loan with an agreement that the country would engage in structural reforms, including cutting back on public sector spending (including the privatisation of loss-making government-owned industries and businesses). However, the Jamaican government and the IMF agreed that government spending on targeted social welfare programmes could increase. An example of this was the school feeding programme, which aims to ensure that all children are provided with nourishing meals at school.

Antigua and Barbuda
Dominica
Grenada
Montserrat
St Kitts and Nevis
St Lucia
St Vincent and the Grenadines

**Associate members**
Anguilla
British Virgin Islands

Members of the Organisation of East Caribbean States

## Free trade

Free trade is trading without barriers such as import tariffs. Countries specialise in what they do most efficiently and then trade with others to buy what they need at a lower cost than manufacturing the products themselves.

Free trade leads to increased prosperity. If countries specialise in their best lines of production, global output of goods and services is increased. Along with economies of scale, more will be produced of better quality and at lower unit cost.

### The World Trade Organisation (WTO)

The WTO was set up in 1995. Its aim is to open up trade for the benefit of all, achieved by rules and agreements set out for trading between nations. Its main principles are:

- to pursue open borders – that is, free trade
- the 'most favoured nation principle': what a country offers to its most favoured trading partner it must also offer to all of its other trading partners, leading to a progressive reduction in tariffs.

### Caribbean Community

CARICOM is a common market of 15 member countries (see 7.4). Its headquarters are in Georgetown, Guyana. Within the Community there is free movement of goods, capital and people. Most goods can be traded between community members without any restrictions. There is a common external tariff (tax) charged by community members on imports from outside the community. The community has also forged a number of bilateral trade deals with other countries, for example Venezuela and Costa Rica. Increasingly the community is seeking to develop even stronger integration, for example in relation to monetary and fiscal policy.

The Caribbean Single Market and Economy (CSME) is a plan put together by members of CARICOM at Grande Anse, Grenada in 1989. The plan included deepening the economic integration between members, widening the membership to more countries, and increasing trade links with other countries.

### European Union

The European Union is an economic and political union consisting of 27 countries, a number of which are part of a single currency union (the Eurozone). The EU has preferential trading agreements with Caribbean countries, allowing a range of agricultural products to enter the EU with zero tariffs.

## African, Caribbean, Pacific group of states (ACP)

The ACP was set up in 1975. It consists of 79 countries, 16 of which are in the Caribbean. Its primary aims are to further the sustainable development of the ACP region, and to reduce poverty. The ACP countries have an economic partnership agreement with the European Union. This agreement recognises that the asymmetrical power relations between these two trading groups – income, output and expenditure levels – are much higher in the EU than in ACP. EU economies also tend to be much larger in terms of population size and geographical area.

The economic partnership agreement therefore gives ACP countries access to EU markets. In 2000 the ACP countries signed the Cotonou Agreement with the EU. This is a 20-year agreement designed to support the development of ACP countries. It includes a plan for development coupled with financial resources to put it into action. The long-term aim is to enable increasing ACP integration into the global economy.

## The Association of Caribbean States (ACS)

The ACS was set up in 1994 and involved 25 Caribbean states. The agreement focused on strengthening regional cooperation and integration between members to improve economic relations, and preserve the environmental wellbeing of the Caribbean Sea, seen as a common resource for all countries in the region. Government ministers from member states meet to discuss areas of common interest.

## The Organisation of Eastern Caribbean States (OECS)

The OECS is an inter-governmental organisation, set up in 1981, seeking to increase the integration and harmonisation of policies of states in the Eastern Caribbean. It also seeks to create joint responsibility for dealing with natural disasters, particularly hurricanes. The Secretariat of the organisation is in Castries, St Lucia. Member states are either full or associate members of the Caribbean Community. The OECS has nine members: Antigua and Barbuda, Dominica, Grenada, Montserrat, St Kitts and Nevis, St Lucia, St Vincent and the Grenadines, Anguilla and the British Virgin Islands. In 2011 a number of these states formed an economic union with Trinidad and Tobago. The key features of OECS are:

- free movement of goods and services and labour
- free movement of capital supervised by the Eastern Caribbean Central Bank
- a common external tariff.

The Eastern Caribbean dollar is the currency unit of the OECS.

# Investment in Caribbean economies

## Foreign direct investment

Foreign direct investment (FDI) is long-term investment in a company that operates in a different country from that in which the investor is based. FDI takes place when the investment gives the investor a controlling interest in the company. The United Nations defines a controlling interest as having 10 per cent or more of the shares.

The motive for such investment is to gain a share of the company's profit. FDI usually involves buying shares in the foreign company or setting up a new company in the country. Foreign direct investment can bring much-needed capital to a country.

Iberostar Suites, Montego Bay, Jamaica: Spanish hotel chains are a source of FDI in many Caribbean countries

---

**CASE STUDY** | Encouraging FDI in Jamaica

Jamaica is one of the prime destinations for FDI into the Caribbean. Typical areas of foreign investment include shipping, call centres and hotels. Jamaica has actively encouraged FDI as a means of creating jobs and prosperity in the country. The Jamaica Promotions Corporation (JAMPRO) was set up by the Jamaican government to encourage FDI. JAMPRO has targeted major European hotel chains, encouraging them to invest. Once these hotel chains invest in the country, several local businesses set up around the new hotel chains. This has a ripple effect, creating prosperity.

**Questions**

**1** Why is Jamaica seeking to encourage FDI?

**2** What are the likely benefits and drawbacks of FDI?

---

Table 7.8.1 summarises some of the benefits and drawbacks of FDI.

**Table 7.8.1** Benefits and drawbacks of FDI

| Benefits of FDI | Drawbacks of FDI |
|---|---|
| An inflow of funds that will be spent in the domestic economy | Foreign investors may come to dominate the domestic market. They may prevent and restrict local competition because economies of scale enable them to operate more efficiently. |
| The likelihood that FDI will be sustained over a period of time | FDI may be withdrawn from a country once the initial advantage of setting up there disappears. |

| Benefits of FDI | Drawbacks of FDI |
|---|---|
| The creation of jobs in the domestic economy | Profits from FDI go to foreign investors. |
| A ripple effect as those that take up the jobs spend their income in the domestic economy | Investors may not be primarily interested in the development of the economy in which they invest. |

## Caribbean Development Bank

The Caribbean Development Bank was set up in 1970 to support the development of member countries in the Caribbean. Assistance for setting up was provided by the United Nations Development Programme and the World Bank. The headquarters is in St Michael, Barbados. The role of the bank is to:

- help borrowing countries to use their resources to improve their economies and to increase trade
- promote investment in the Caribbean
- bring in financial resources from within the Caribbean and outside to support development
- support the development of financial institutions in the Caribbean.

The bank is run very carefully and has a very high reputation and an excellent credit rating. It has substantial reserves available for development projects.

**KEY POINTS**

- Foreign direct investment is investment by foreign investors giving them a controlling interest in overseas enterprises.
- The Caribbean Development Bank's role is to provide funds to help support the development of individual states within the Caribbean and in the area as a whole.

**SUMMARY QUESTIONS**

1 What is foreign direct investment?

2 Why does foreign investment take place?

3 How is foreign direct investment both a benefit and an issue for Caribbean countries and businesses?

# Preferential tariff arrangements

Bananas in the Caribbean tend to be grown on relatively small plantations compared with rivals in Latin America

## What is protection?

Trade protection means restricting the entry of foreign goods into a domestic market, or imposing a tax to raise the price of imports. The purpose of these restrictions is to protect domestic industries. Governments may do this by:

• restricting the number of imports
• making imports more expensive by taxing them
• limiting the availability of foreign exchange required to purchase them.

### Preferential tariffs

Tariffs are import taxes. The impact of governments levying import taxes is to distort trade patterns. Imported goods that have tariffs levied on them become more expensive and therefore less attractive to buyers. Where a government imposes lower tariffs on some imports and higher tariffs on others, the lower tariffs are preferential tariffs. A good example of preferential tariffs was the zero or lower tariff regime that the UK applied to Commonwealth countries. However, when the UK joined the European Union in 1973 this preferential arrangement was threatened. The European Union has a common external tariff.

### EXAM TIP

Make sure you are familiar with the main purpose of providing preferential tariffs, that is to tax the imports of preferred countries at lower rates than those of other countries. This gives the preferred nation a competitive advantage over some or all of its rivals.

| CASE STUDY | Banana wars |
| --- | --- |

The 'banana wars' have raged for decades. The European Union has consistently applied preferential tariffs to a range of agricultural products from ACP countries including bananas. However, these tariffs have been opposed by Latin American banana growers and the huge North American companies, Chiquita and Dole, which dominate the banana market. These critics of preferential banana tariffs have taken their case to the World Trade Organisation and there has been continuing pressure on the EU to reduce tariff barriers faced by non-ACAP banana growers.

Caribbean bananas tend to be grown by smallholders in the Windward Islands. Sales of bananas are central to these economies, and preferential tariffs have enabled the Eastern Caribbean to have access to European markets. However, tariffs imposed on Latin American bananas have steadily been reduced so that by 2011 they were virtually eliminated.

Criticisms of preferential tariffs have been that:

• they discriminate against more efficient producers

- they have made some regions over-reliant on protection from preferential treatment, rather than diversifying their economies.

In a global economy dominated by large-scale producers, however, it is very difficult for small island economies to diversify to produce other goods.

**Questions**

**1** What is the purpose behind preferential tariffs?

**2** What are the advantages and drawbacks of having preferential tariffs?

## Reasons for granting preferential tariffs

The Generalised System of Preferences (GSPs) is a non-reciprocal preferential tariff scheme applied to most products. The idea of creating preferential tariffs was first justified in 1964 by Raul Prebisch, Secretary General of the United Nations Committee for Trade and Development (UNCTAD). Prebisch argued that the smaller domestic markets of developing countries and their less developed resources necessitated support and access to international markets to create fairer conditions for all. From 1968 GSP was established. Today GSP schemes recognised by UNCTAD mean that many Caribbean products have tariff-free access to markets in the United States, Canada and the European Union. The non-reciprocal nature of the agreement means that Caribbean economies are not obliged to offer preferential tariffs on imports from these nations.

**KEY POINTS**

- A preferential tariff is a lower level of import tax for some countries than is allowed for imports from other countries.
- The Caribbean region benefits from a number of preferential tariff arrangements with trading partners. However, these are steadily being removed.

**SUMMARY QUESTIONS**

1 What is a preferential tariff?

2 Give two examples of Caribbean exports that have received preferential tariff treatment in recent years.

3 How do preferential tariff arrangements help Caribbean exporters?

# The benefits and costs of preferential trade

Candidates should be able to:

- identify the benefits and costs associated with CARICOM's participation in preferential trade arrangements.

While preferential trade can provide benefits by giving a trading advantage to a preferred partner, in the longer term it may have the harmful effect of discouraging the partner from developing new lines and products with which it could develop comparative advantage in the future.

**Figure 7.10.1** Cinnamon, ginger and nutmeg, Dominica: preferential trading arrangements help producers of such items in the domestic economy

## The benefits of preferential trade

Caribbean economies have benefited from preferential trading arrangements in a number of ways:

- increased interaction in international markets
- being able to be more competitive in selling their products in the markets where they are given preferential treatment
- being able to sustain small-scale production, enabling the creation of employment for smallholders and other producers in the domestic economy
- having a guaranteed steady export market, for example where Caribbean exporters are guaranteed a fixed quota of sales, such as sugar into the European Union
- the development of good relations with partners, for example continued Commonwealth ties with the UK and Canada.

## The drawbacks of preferential trade

However, there are a number of drawbacks associated with preferential trade.

- Preferential trade creates dependency on the preferential arrangements. When a business is not competitive it is usually forced to close. However, preferential arrangements made some producers artificially competitive. The preferential arrangements were set within a time frame – 20 years in some instances. When the agreements come to an end, the dependent producers have not always prepared themselves for this change.
- The dependency discourages innovation and some Caribbean economies have failed to diversify in a way that would have supported longer-term growth.

• Buyers in countries that offer preferential arrangements have to pay higher prices for goods.

## Economic Partnership Agreements

Preferential trade arrangements have been criticised by the World Trade Organisation as being unfair to non-participating countries. As a result trade groups such as the European Union and NAFTA have sought to develop new relationships with the African, Caribbean and Pacific group of countries. Economic partnerships are being suggested as a way forward.

An economic partnership agreement is reciprocal – that is, it is a two-way trading arrangement. It is also non-discriminatory: it does not favour one country or group of countries. These two aspects, reciprocity and non-discrimination, are in line with the WTO rules. Economic Partnership Agreements are open to all developing countries, not just ACP countries.

Developing countries have been encouraged to enter into Economic Partnership Agreements with the EU in regional groups. The regional group that applies to the Caribbean is CARIFORUM: the Caribbean Community with the Dominican Republic.

Economic Partnership Agreements are designed to be phased in, giving ACP countries between 15 and 25 years to open up their markets to imports from the European Union. These agreements increasingly move Caribbean economies towards a free trade area with partner countries.

Some Caribbean countries are opposed to Economic Partnership Agreements: rum producers, for example, see the agreement as a threat to their long-term prosperity as their markets are exposed to increasing international competition.

**KEY POINTS**

• Preferential trade arrangements provide favoured countries with more secure markets, and the possibility of competing on price with more efficient rivals.

• Preferential trade arrangements tend to cushion those countries and producers that are protected, whereas there might be greater benefit more from being competitive and having to diversify.

**SUMMARY QUESTIONS**

1 Choose a Caribbean country and list five benefits that it receives from preferential tariff arrangements when exporting to the European Union.

2 Explain three drawbacks to the same economy of such preferential tariff arrangements.

# Trade liberalisation

The World Trade Organisation creates rules and frameworks for international trade and seeks to reduce tariffs and quotas

## What is trade liberalisation?

Trade liberalisation is the process of opening up trade between nations by the removal of restrictions. The World Trade Organisation (WTO) is involved in progressive rounds of talks to encourage the liberalisation of world trade.

Arguments in favour of trade liberalisation, based on specialisation following the principles of comparative advantage, are that the growth of the world economy and the volume of trade will increase, and greater prosperity will result.

Arguments against trade liberalisation are that it benefits rich countries that have been able to develop comparative advantage in high-value-added products. Less developed countries are not able to compete and the result is greater dependency and debt.

## The WTO and trade liberalisation

The WTO is made up of over 150 countries negotiating trade deals aimed at progressively liberalising trade. The WTO is currently negotiating the 'Doha Round', talks designed to encourage developing countries to open up their economies. These talks have been ongoing since 2001, but there has been considerable disagreement between the United States and other groups of countries, led by India and China. One of the major points of dispute is the protection by the United States of its own agricultural industry and the provision of subsidies to farmers who export products such as grain. In many developing countries 75 per cent or more of the working population is engaged in agriculture, but US farm subsidies makes it difficult to export to the United States. Other countries are therefore reluctant to open up their own economies by reducing import tariffs.

**DID YOU KNOW?**

Sugar has largely been left out of the Doha Round of trade liberalisation talks. Sugar production is subsidised in the European Union and the United States. Sugar producers in countries such as India believe that removing tariff subsidies would give greater access for their sugar growers to lucrative world markets.

## The benefits of trade liberalisation

In a world with perfectly free trade, countries and regions would specialise on lines in which they have the greatest comparative advantage. Economists argue that this would lead to the most efficient use of resources, in turn leading to economic growth and prosperity and the least waste of resources. Through competition countries would be forced to concentrate on their best lines and cut out less efficient production.

## The costs of trade liberalisation

The most efficient producers would benefit and this would particularly benefit developed countries. Developing countries might lose out from:

- deteriorating terms of trade
- increased poverty
- increased inequality
- dependency on borrowing – so that governments are less able to pursue their own development strategies.

## Managing trade liberalisation

Trade liberalisation in the right circumstances can be an important means to securing development. However, imposing trade liberalisation on economies before they are ready can slow down or destroy development. Trade liberalisation needs to be managed in such a way that markets are open to trade competition only when they are developed enough to compete.

Many countries' experience of liberalisation is that it can be harmful when it is not properly managed. For example, the reduction in preferential tariffs for banana exporters in the Windward Islands has led to high levels of poverty and unemployment in some areas. Less developed Caribbean economies need to be able to protect their fragile industries rather than being rushed into a world in which they have no protection.

**KEY POINTS**

- Trade liberalisation is the process whereby countries open up their markets to international trade.
- Trade liberalisation leads to specialisation along the lines of comparative advantage.
- Trade liberalisation can be harmful when a country's industries are not at an appropriate level of development to withstand competition.

**SUMMARY QUESTIONS**

1 What is trade liberalisation?

2 Who is likely to be in favour of trade liberalisation?

3 What benefits and what drawbacks does liberalisation present for the Caribbean?

# The benefits of globalisation

Jamaican Blue Mountain coffee can be found on sale across the world and is instantly recognised by coffee connoisseurs

## The nature of globalisation

In a global economy goods can be produced in many different places and transported for sale to destinations on the other side of the world. Globalisation involves the free movement of goods, capital, labour and technology. Globalisation involves intense competition because products and resources can be transferred and brought to market all over the world.

| **CASE STUDY** | Jamaican Blue Mountain coffee |
| --- | --- |

Blue Mountain coffee has been grown in Jamaica for over 300 years. It is a variety of coffee that can only be grown in Jamaica. It has a mild flavour, no bitterness and a relatively low caffeine content. Its supply is determined by the amount of land in which it can be cultivated. It is therefore highly sought after across the world and fetches premium prices.

As a global product the coffee has extensive reach: it takes a 16-hour flight to transport the coffee from Kingston to Tokyo, but the fact that 80 per cent of the coffee is distributed to Japan shows that distance is no object in a global economy. In Japan, Blue Mountain coffee competes with other internationally grown coffees from Brazil, Colombia, Kenya and many other countries, but it is carefully branded and marketed to ensure that it is competitive in the global marketplace. The Coffee Industry Board of Jamaica carefully monitors the production and sale of the coffee to make sure that it meets the high standards expected on global markets. The resulting global product is instantly recognised and valued across the world. The coffee can also be purchased online.

### Questions

**1** In what way is Blue Mountain coffee a global product?

**2** What is the competition for Blue Mountain coffee?

Globalisation involves a number of interrelated concepts. A key feature is that products, people and capital are highly mobile. Shops in the Caribbean stock products sourced from all over the globe, and products from the Caribbean are exported across the world. People travel to and from the Caribbean as students, business managers, technical workers, researchers and tourists. Foreigners invest in Caribbean enterprises, and people from the Caribbean invest overseas.

Globalisation provides both challenges and opportunities for Caribbean economies. A major challenge is the scale of the competition facing Caribbean-based businesses. Multinational companies from the United States, Europe, China, Brazil, India and elsewhere have huge domestic markets enabling them to benefit from large-scale production and distribution. Inevitably this drives down their costs. Global companies are able to spread their marketing, advertising and production costs across global sales.

However, globalisation also provides real opportunities. Caribbean entrepreneurs can set up **joint ventures** with overseas partners – that is, new businesses with capital and input both from the owners of existing Caribbean enterprises, and the owners of foreign enterprises. The Caribbean entrepreneur brings local knowledge and contacts, while the foreign partner provides additional capital and access to global markets. Alternatively Caribbean enterprises can access the global market through the internet, which is an unparalleled medium for selling niche regional products to a global market.

## The benefits of large-scale production of goods

Globalisation offers large companies the opportunity of exploiting vast economies of scale. Large car companies are able to produce vehicles on a huge scale, such as in the car plants in Brazil and Mexico where land and labour are relatively cheap. Standard advertising and marketing literature can be used and the companies are then able to market these products through dealerships throughout the Americas and the Caribbean region. Manufacturers of people-carrier vehicles such as Japan's Toyota and Germany's Volkswagen produce models that can be used as taxis throughout the Caribbean (there is a Toyota dealership in practically every Caribbean territory) and elsewhere across the globe. Like Blue Mountain coffee and Red Stripe beer, Toyota and Volkswagen are globally recognised products.

Large scale production enables:

- low-cost mass production
- low-cost mass advertising and marketing
- competitive pricing
- global recognition
- mass sales.

**SUMMARY QUESTIONS**

1 Outline four key features of globalisation.

2 How is globalisation likely to lead to greater specialisation and economies of scale?

3 What are the benefits of large-scale global production?

# The effects of globalisation and trade liberalisation

## LEARNING OUTCOME

Candidates should be able to:

- state the effects of globalisation and trade liberalisation on territories, firms, consumers and governments in the Caribbean.

Trade liberalisation has led to a flood of cheap textiles from China

## The impact of global markets

Previous chapters in this unit have identified some of the major realities facing Caribbean economies in the early 21st century, resulting from trade liberalisation and globalisation:

- Markets are increasingly open to international competition and there are fewer preferential tariffs.
- Relatively small Caribbean economies and producers are having to compete with much larger non-Caribbean economies and producers.
- Caribbean companies that export typically engage in relatively small-scale production, whereas many imports to the Caribbean are produced on a vast scale by multinational companies.

| CASE STUDY | The sugar and banana industries: the impact of globalisation |
|---|---|

In 2001, Belal Ahmed, an agricultural consultant at the University of the West Indies, published a paper looking at the impact of globalisation on the sugar and banana industries. His paper was particularly important because it looked at the impact of globalisation on the Caribbean's two major foreign exchange earners and principal sources of employment. At the time he reported that the cost of production of sugar and bananas was three times higher than the world market price. He showed that this was only possible to maintain through preferential trading arrangements granted to the Caribbean zone. He warned that once these guarantees disappeared, Caribbean producers would be subject to the full force of the impact of globalisation.

The problem caused by reliance on sugar and bananas was that production and productivity was difficult to increase, there was a lack of opportunity for economies of scale and low levels of technology in these industries. Ahmed also pointed out that little value was being added to these products to enable them to yield higher profit margins.

Solutions suggested for these difficulties included closing down some loss-making enterprises and diversifying economies to include the growth of tourism, information technology and agricultural processing industries. To make these changes Ahmed stressed the importance of stable economic, social and political conditions to encourage foreign investment. He also argued that Caribbean governments should put pressure on the United Nations to have Caribbean islands recognised as 'Small States' and thus able to benefit from appropriate financial assistance for development.

## Impact on territories

The impact of trade liberalisation has been most severe for the parts of the Caribbean, such as the Windward Islands, that depend on one or a very narrow range of exports. Larger economies such as Trinidad, Jamaica, Guyana and Barbados have been far more successful at diversifying their economies and developing new growth industries such as tourism, which benefit from the opening up of markets.

The worst-hit economies are suffering from a lack of productive capital and the export of capital to pay interest payments on debts. As agricultural industries decline, there are high levels of structural unemployment and falling standards of living for large numbers of people.

## Impact on firms

Businesses in the agricultural sector, particularly sugar and banana production, have been hit hard by trade liberalisation. However, as we saw in 7.12, other businesses such as Blue Mountain coffee exporters in Jamaica have benefited. Firms in new growth sectors such as tourism have flourished. Businesses have been able to benefit from inflows of foreign capital. However, many large businesses, for example large tourist hotel chains, are partly or fully owned by overseas companies.

## Impact on consumers

Consumers benefit from the ready availability of products from all round the globe. Many of these, such as cheap textile garments produced in China, are relatively cheap as a result of mass production. However, consumers need to have a steady income in order to benefit from goods provided in the global market. For the poorest sections of the community, prices of global branded products are often too expensive.

## Impact on governments

Many governments have become more dependent on overseas financial backing. Access to the global economy exposes nations to sharp rises and falls in economic fortunes. In times of crisis governments have to borrow from the International Monetary Fund and other lenders who can then impose structural adjustment programmes. Governments are also dependent on foreign multinationals to provide jobs. Globalisation and trade liberalisation therefore reduce the power of national governments to make economic decisions.

# Benefits of CARICOM

Blue waters bottled water from Trinidad is exported widely within CARICOM

**EXAM TIP**

When answering questions about the benefits of CARICOM, make sure you can explain how the revised Treaty of Chaguamaras helps to provide a way forward for integrating the economies of Caribbean countries, so that collectively they are able to have more strength than if they were to work as individual states.

The revised Treaty of Chaguaramas established the Caribbean Community in 2001. The Community should be seen as a measure to integrate the regional economy in order to create an economic system that collectively will be able to survive and prosper in a global economy. By working together, Caribbean states are able to integrate their production system in order to make best use of available resources. The Caribbean Community should be seen as a 'work in progress' rather than a finished article.

The revised Treaty established many objectives including:

• diversifying agriculture and developing new agro-industries that would add value to existing agricultural production

• developing land, air and maritime transport

• creating a macro-economic environment that will encourage outside investment in the CARICOM area

• maximising productive efficiency in the region, particularly with a view to gaining valuable foreign exchange earnings

• focusing on market-led production of goods and services

• unleashing the power of small business enterprises

• providing a transitional phase for less developed members of the Community, to enable them to catch up and be more competitive with other members

• developing suitable methods of resolving disputes between member states.

## The four freedoms

A key aspect of CARICOM is the Caribbean Single Market and Economy (CSME). This involves four freedoms. These are set out in Figure 7.14.1.

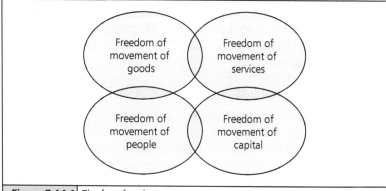

**Figure 7.14.1** The four freedoms

It is important to be familiar with the social and economic benefits of these four freedoms. The key economic benefits are as follows:

- Increased trade enables countries to specialise in producing goods in which they have greatest comparative advantage. Scarce resources are allocated to lines of production in which an economy has the least opportunity cost. Thus the combined output of the CARICOM members increases.
- Access to a larger regional market enables producers in member countries to benefit from economies of scale – for example St Vincent and Trinidad are able to export bottled water on a large scale to tourist islands, as well as to sell on cruise ships.
- The removal of trade barriers leads to cross-border competition. This can lead to lower prices of goods and encourages businesses to be innovative in seeking to cut costs. For example, the telecommunications industry is highly competitive, as is inter-island transport in many areas.
- Companies that previously saw themselves as being Trinidadian, Guyanese or Jamaican may now see themselves as Caribbean, competing in a global market place. Examples are Caribbean Passion Inc. (a company specialising in carnivals in the Caribbean and across the globe) and Island Routes Caribbean Adventure Tours.

The social benefits of the Single Market and Economy include:

- shared responsibility for common problems such as dealing with the impacts of hurricane damage, and more developed regions of CARICOM supporting development in less developed areas
- shared participation by people across the Caribbean in working together as a social and cultural community.

The revised Treaty set out that 'Member States commit themselves to the goal of the free movement of their nationals within the community'. The benefit of such movement is that countries and employers are able to recruit the best people to work with their existing resources, which will help to increase productivity in individual states and in the community as a whole. Employees benefit in that they are able to secure work in places where they can gain the greatest economic and personal advantage.

The benefit of the free movement of capital is that Caribbean citizens are able to invest their capital in projects and territories that will yield the highest returns within CARICOM. This should lead to the greatest return on capital. Currencies are also freely exchangeable within the Community, helping to reduce the cost of business activity within CARICOM.

## DID YOU KNOW?

The free movement of people is still restricted except for graduates, media persons, artists, musicians and certain categories of sports persons, such as high-grade cricketers and coaches. There is also free movement of certain grades of managers, researchers and technical workers.

## KEY POINTS

- The revised Treaty of Chaguaramas provides a 'road map' for greater integration of the Caribbean regional economy.
- Economic benefits include increased specialisation leading to more effective large-scale output at lower cost.
- Social benefits include greater cooperation and mutual support.

## SUMMARY QUESTIONS

1 What is the purpose of the Caribbean Single Market and Economy?

2 What benefits is it bringing to its members?

# Development strategies in the Caribbean

Garment manufacture, Jamaica: textile factories have been set up in Kingston as part of an export push process

## Alternative strategies

During the 1980s and 1990s, many Caribbean economies focused on moving away from dependence on agriculture to try to develop their own industries and reduce expensive imports of finished goods. There was a strong emphasis on industrialisation by invitation and import substitution. The Caribbean has become more service-oriented with the emphasis on diversification and integration, and export push.

Figure 7.15.1 shows the four main economic strategies that Caribbean governments can apply to regional development. Each of these strategies is designed to tackle problems associated with:

• the development gap between Caribbean economies and huge competing economies in a global market place, for example the United States, the EU, India, Brazil, Russia and China

• foreign debt, dependency and the need for foreign currency.

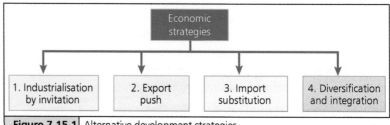

**Figure 7.15.1** Alternative development strategies

## Industrialisation by invitation

A major strategy for the development of the Caribbean has been to invite (or allow) overseas companies to invest in plant and facilities. The overseas company brings with it a lot of capital and then creates jobs. ALCOA has operated for many years in Jamaica where it extracts aluminium. More recently Spanish hotel chains such as Iberostar and Riu have set up in Jamaica and in other parts of the Caribbean. Whereas aluminium production is capital intensive (creating relatively few jobs), the hotel industry is labour intensive. However, the sheer scale of the new hotel developments poses a threat to existing local companies such as Sandals. Today, the Caribbean attracts large sums of foreign capital from new investors, including major investments by China.

## Export push

The Caribbean area imports large quantities of manufactured products as well as food and services. Caribbean states therefore need to earn foreign currency to balance international payments. One approach to development has been through policies known as 'export push'. This involves the development of industries specifically for export. In the 1980s Jamaica developed food processing and garment exporting industries largely targeted at the US market, and a range of factories was set up in Kingston and other large towns in Jamaica. More recently most Caribbean economies have focused on export push strategies through the development of tourism.

---

**CASE STUDY** | Exporting water

In 2009 the government of Dominica granted an American company, Sisserou Water Inc., the rights to capture and export water for export from the Clyde River. Over 13 billion litres of water will be captured each year. Criticism of this project is that it will interfere with the natural resource systems of the river, leading to ecological destruction. The development of the project will lead initially to the creation of 25 jobs in Dominica.

### Questions

**1** In what ways can this project be seen as one leading to development?

**2** In what ways can this project be seen as one that works against development?

---

## Import substitution

During the 1980s and 1990s Import Substitution Industrialisation (ISI) was used as a development strategy by many countries in the region. The rationale was that this approach would counteract dependency. At the time Caribbean economies focused on selling low-value-added commodities such as sugar and bananas to world markets. ISI involves countries building their own industries, such as food-processing industries. Once businesses start to process food and other manufactured goods they can begin to brand them, making them more valuable to the end consumer. Caribbean countries started to develop chemical-processing industries, agricultural fertiliser industries, textile, shoe and many other types of production. ISI was accompanied by tariff protection to protect these new industries from cheaper foreign imports. Today ISI has fewer supporters because it is seen to distort specialisation along the lines of comparative advantage.

## Diversification and integration

The topics in Section 7 have shown that current strategies in the Caribbean for development focus on integration of Caribbean nations into a regional bloc – the Caribbean Community. Creating this regional trading bloc is seen as a way of creating greater economies of scale based on trade liberalisation within the Caribbean. This will enable the economies to compete more successfully and become less dependent on partners from outside the region. This strategy is coupled with measures to diversify economies – particularly by developing tourism, information technology, media, cultural and sports-related industries. Other examples of diversification include the development of ecotourism in various parts of the region.

**KEY POINTS**

- Industrialisation by invitation involved bringing in foreign capital and companies.
- Export push focused on developing export industries.
- Import substitution involved replacing industrial imports with home-grown products
- Integration and diversification is the current development strategy supported by CARICOM.

**SUMMARY QUESTIONS**

1 Compare the relative advantages of export push, industrialisation by invitation, and diversification and integration.

2 Which of these policies is most likely to be successful in an era of trade liberalisation?

E-commerce enables 24-hour electronic selling

Source: From www.barbados.org. An AXSES website © AXSES SCI, 1995–2009

## What is e-commerce?

E-commerce involves using electronic means (typically the internet) to trade. It is the most rapidly growing area of the international economy. To engage in e-commerce a business needs to create (or have someone create) a website, which is then put online using the services of an internet service provider. The site needs to be reliable, accessible 24 hours a day, and have the following qualities:

• It should be easy to use and to navigate.

• Consumers using the site must be able to view accurate depictions and read accurate descriptions of goods and services that are for sale.

• Payment should be secure and the process easy to carry out.

There are a number of forms of e-commerce:

• B2C commerce (business-to-customer): a business such as a retailer or manufacturer sells goods to the end consumer, for example buying fashion clothes online.

• B2B commerce (business-to-business): a business such as a supplier of engineering components sells engineering parts to vehicle manufacturers.

• C2C commerce (customer-to-customer): one person sells goods to others, for example selling some of your compact discs to someone else who wants to purchase them.

## The benefits of e-commerce

There are a number of benefits to companies and countries that develop online commerce:

• Access to a wider market: the possibility for economies of scale in any business depends on the extent of the market. E-commerce provides potential access to a global market. People anywhere in the world can make a reservation for a hotel in Grenada.

• Lower costs of production: a business can benefit from lower fixed costs and lower variable costs from operating online. Instead of requiring a 'bricks and mortar' selling outlet, goods sold online can be stored in a warehouse at any location. The initial fixed costs are setting up an online presence, which can be costly, but once these have been 'sunk' into the start-up or development of the business they can then be spread over a very large output. Variable costs are also lower because the cost per extra unit produced will be lower than for a 'bricks and mortar' business, with less labour and other resource inputs likely to be required.

• Customers are able to make purchases from their own home and in their own time. Purchases can be made 24 hours a day, regardless of time zones.

## Issues involved in setting up an e-commerce site

A country's ability to engage in e-commerce depends on the quality and availability of internet services in that country. The Caribbean area is fortunate to have particularly good access.

There are a number of issues associated with setting up an online presence. These include the quality of the technology involved and the reliability of the service. Intermittent internet access means fewer opportunities for effective e-commerce. In the Caribbean the key issues relate to being able to connect to the internet (for example in some rural areas there may be relatively poor access) and security of payment.

### Factors leading to success

E-commerce provides a real opportunity for Caribbean economies because it provides a link to a global audience. Caribbean governments have sought to develop the IT sector through provision of training opportunities and encouragement of foreign multinationals to set up high-quality broadband networks.

For entrepreneurs wishing to set up e-commerce sites the challenges are to ensure that:

- the website design is good, with ease of navigation through sites, leading to the purchase and closure of the sale
- loading of the website is rapid
- information on the site is accurate and up to date
- when customers place orders, the response is swift
- privacy of customer information is secure
- it is possible to complete a transaction: the purchaser should be able to pay quickly and receive a response stating that their order has been received and payment processed.

### Government measures to develop e-commerce

Caribbean governments are keen to increase the growth of the IT sector of the economy, particularly in relation to the development of e-commerce. E-commerce is seen as an important means to link both small and larger Caribbean businesses to the international market. Government initiatives include the subsidy of e-learning facilities in schools and universities, and the provision of government training schemes for business people and others to develop e-commerce capabilities and other business skills. Governments also work closely with internet service providers to develop strong networks of internet connections to link up users in their economies to the global market place. Governments also provide workshops to introduce entrepreneurs to the benefits of e-commerce.

**SUMMARY QUESTIONS**

1 What is e-commerce?

2 What are the main advantages to Caribbean economies of engaging in e-commerce?

3 What are the barriers to developing effective e-commerce in the Caribbean?

## SECTION 1: Multiple-choice questions

1 Trade liberalisation is most likely to harm a Caribbean economy which:

   a Is dependent on a single export that benefits from preferential tariffs

   b Has a strong comparative advantage in key export industries

   c Engages in very little international trade

   d Already engages in virtually free trade with its trade partners

2 Which of the following is *not* a feature of the Caribbean Single Market and Economy?

   a Freedom of movement of goods

   b Freedom of movement of people

   c A common external tariff

   d A common currency

3 The policy of import substitution used by a number of Caribbean economies was designed to:

   a Increase the level of imports by Caribbean economies

   b Reduce dependency in Caribbean economies

   c Substitute low-value imports for high-value imports

   d Substitute exports with imports

4 A key benefit to Caribbean companies from engaging in e-commerce is that:

   a This will raise their long-term costs while reducing their short-term costs

   b This will give them access to a wider international market

   c They will be able to raise the prices that they charge for goods

   d They will not need to invest in new technologies

5 One of the major goals of the World Trade Organisation (WTO) is to:

   a Encourage trade deals that progressively liberalise trade

   b Create international payment systems that enhance trade

   c Provide funds for countries with balance of payments problems

   d Encourage trading blocs to establish tariff barriers to restrict trade

6 Which of the following is not a feature of CARICOM?

   a Free exchange of currencies between member states

   b Shared responsibility for dealing with hurricane damage

   c A commitment to the goal of free movement of nationals between members

   d A commitment to non-competition between companies in member states

7 Which of the following is a cost of trade liberalisation to Caribbean economies?

   a Reductions in inequality

   b Reduced dependency on borrowing

   c Deteriorating terms of trade

   d Increased specialisation based on comparative advantage

8 Which of the following is a criticism of the activities of multinational corporations operating in the Caribbean?

   a They have introduced complex new technologies

   b They have engaged in foreign direct investment

   c They repatriate the majority of profits made in the area

   d They support new training initiatives

9 A criticism of globalisation and trade liberalisation is that:

  a  It primarily benefits countries whose comparative advantage is in high-value-added products

  b  Specialisation on the lines of comparative advantage increases levels of world output

  c  It gives smaller countries greater access to the markets of larger economies

  d  It enables greater movement of capital, goods and services on a global scale

10 Which of the following trading areas is based on a widely functioning common currency unit involving most members?

  a  ACP          b  ACS

  c  OECS       d  CARICOM

## SECTION 2: Structured questions

1 a  Describe three key economic characteristics of Caribbean economies. (*6 marks*)

  b  Explain two ways in which Caribbean economies benefit from being members of CARICOM. (*4 marks*)

  c  Outline the concept of trade liberalisation. (*5 marks*)

2 a  Define the term *debt burden*. (*2 marks*)

  b  Describe the relationship between the debt burden and dependency in Caribbean economies. (*5 marks*)

  c  Describe two policies that Caribbean economies have used to try to free themselves from the debt burden. (*4 marks*)

  d  Explain two of the benefits of one of these policies. (*4 marks*)

3 a  Define globalisation. (*2 marks*)

  b  Describe three resources that Caribbean economies have that enable them to compete in a globalised economy. (*6 marks*)

  c  Explain one way in which the work of the International Monetary Fund (IMF) provides help to Caribbean economies in a globalised world economy. (*3 marks*)

  d  How might protectionism help Caribbean economies in a globalised economy? (*4 marks*)

4 a  Describe two shared features of CARICOM and the European Union in terms of economic integration. (*4 marks*)

  b  Describe one difference between the European Union and CARICOM in terms of economic integration. (*2 marks*)

  c  Explain three benefits to Caribbean economies engaged in trade liberalisation. (*6 marks*)

  d  How does the World Trade Organisation seek to develop trade liberalisation? (*2 marks*)

5 a  Explain the main difference between bilateral and multilateral trade agreements. (*2 marks*)

  b  Identify one multilateral trade agreement that operates within the Caribbean area and explain how it operates. (*3 marks*)

  c  Explain two ways in which the World Bank supports Caribbean economies. (*4 marks*)

  d  What are preferential tariffs? (*2 marks*)

# Glossary

## A

**Abnormal profit:** the profit that a business makes in excess of the profit required to satisfy the owners that they should remain in that line of business

**Appreciation:** a rise in the value of the currency in terms of other currencies for which it can be exchanged (applies to flexible exchange rate systems only)

**Average cost:** the total cost of producing a given output divided by the number of units produced

**Average fixed cost:** the total fixed cost divided by the number of units produced

**Average total cost (ATC):** total cost of production of any given output divided by the number of units sold; also referred to as average cost (AC)

**Average variable cost (AVC):** calculated by dividing the total variable cost by the number of units of production

## B

**Balance of payments:** account setting out financial flows resulting from a country's trading and financial exchanges with other countries

**Balance of trade:** difference between the monetary value of exports and imports of a country in a given period of time

**Balance of trade account:** account recording monetary values of exports and imports in a country in a given period of time

**Base rate:** the rate of interest set by the central bank on which other financial institutions set their own interest rates. Other financial institutions charge a higher rate than the base rate

**Base year:** a year used as a basis for comparison when creating an index. The base year is given a figure of 100. Comparisons can then be made against the base year (e.g. 110 would represent a figure 10 per cent higher than the base figure)

**Broker members:** members of the stock exchange who trade in shares on the behalf of third parties

## C

**Capital:** refers to items that go into further production (e.g. machines, factory buildings). Can also be used to refer to the finance acquired by a business to pay for its activities

**Central bank:** a country's main monetary authority (e.g. the Eastern Caribbean Central Bank), which controls the supply of money and supervises other banks

**Ceteris paribus:** Latin expression meaning 'holding all other things the same'. This makes it possible to identify the relationship between two factors while holding all other factors constant

**Choice:** opportunity to select from alternative end products and between alternative actions

**Comparative advantage:** being relatively more efficient at certain activities compared with others that can be carried out using the same resources

**Complementary goods:** goods demanded for use together (e.g. laptop computers and the computer software that can be installed on them)

**Consumer Price Index (CPI):** measure of the change over time in the cost of a fixed basket of goods and services, including food, housing, transport and electricity

**Contraction in supply/demand:** decrease in quantity demanded or supplied resulting solely from change in the price

**Cost-push inflation:** general rise in prices resulting from increases in production costs, such as an increase in the price of imported raw materials or energy

**Cross-price elasticity:** measure of responsiveness of change in demand for one good as a result of a change in the price of another good

**Current account (chequing account):** bank account that enables an account holder to deposit and withdraw sums and make payments using their bank card. The account holder pays interest on negative balances

**Cyclical unemployment:** unemployment resulting from downturns in the trade cycle (i.e. when there is a general fall in demand in an economy)

## D

**Debt burden:** legacy of foreign debt that results in interest payments and repayments of capital having to be paid out of current GDP

**Deed of partnership:** formal written agreement setting out the legal arrangements of a partnership

**Demand-pull inflation:** general rise in prices resulting from a general increase in the demand for goods in an economy

**Dependency situation:** where the management of an economy is constrained by reliance on other foreign nations or institutions

**Depreciation:** fall in the value of an international currency on international exchange markets (applies to flexible exchange rate systems only)

**Devaluation:** where a government sets a new lower price for the domestic currency in terms of other exchange currencies so that the prices of a country's goods become more competitive in international markets

**Developed country/economy:** country characterised by relatively high GDP per head and HDI indicators, low birth and death rates, allowing 'all … citizens to enjoy a free and healthy life in a safe environment' (Kofi Annan, former Secretary General, UN)

**Developing country/economy:** low- or middle-income country, characterised by lower levels of GDP per head and industrialisation, with higher birth and death rates than developed countries (World Bank definition)

**Direct tax:** compulsory payment that has to be made without any intermediary (e.g. by the income earner – income tax – or the householder – government rates) (cf Indirect tax)

**Disposable income:** money available for spending after tax and other compulsory deductions

**Division of labour:** concentration of workers on specific specialist work tasks

## E

**Economic growth:** the increased efficiency of an economy to produce goods over time, measured by rising GDP

**Economic good:** a good that is scarce relative to the demand for it

**Economic rent:** the reward to the owners of land

**Economies of scale:** advantages of a larger firm over a smaller, enabling it to produce larger outputs at lower unit costs

**Elastic:** the demand or supply of a good is said to be elastic over a given price range when the change in quantity demanded or supplied is of a greater proportion than an initial price change

**Equilibrium price:** the price at which quantity demanded equals quantity supplied to a market, and at which demanders and suppliers are content

**European Union:** an economic and political union between (in 2011) 27 countries. These countries have signed the

# Glossary

treaties governing the set-up and running of the union and are bound by the laws established by this body. The EU is a free trade area and common market with close historical links to the Caribbean

**Exchange rate regime:** any system of establishing the exchange value of international currencies; variations include fixed exchange rates and floating exchange rates

**Extension in supply/demand:** an increase in the quantity demanded or supplied resulting solely from the change in the price of that good

## F

**Factors of production:** resources used in production: land, labour, capital and enterprise

**Financial instruments:** means of financial transaction, usually a document giving legal rights and obligations (e.g. government bills, bonds or mortgage documents, as well as bank notes or cheques)

**Fiscal policy:** deliberately adjusting the relationship between government taxes and spending in order to achieve government policy objectives

**Fixed asset:** an asset that is normally kept within an organisation over a long period of time to generate income (e.g. a factory building or machine)

**Fixed costs:** any costs that do not vary with the level of output (e.g. rent and rates)

**Fixed exchange rate:** established rate at which one currency will exchange for another. The government can fix the exchange rate between its currency and one or more other currencies; this is difficult to maintain over time

**Floating exchange rate:** an exchange rate between one currency and others determined by their relative demand and supply; it changes from day to day

**Free good:** a good that is in such abundant supply that no sacrifice has to be made to obtain it. There is no opportunity cost associated with its use

## G

**Globalisation:** process of increasing connectedness and similarity of international markets and institutions resulting from increased international communication and exchange

**Government bond:** paper document representing a loan to the government often repayable at a certain date in the future.

The holder of the bond receives interest at regular intervals

**Government deficit:** extent of government overspending compared with revenues received (e.g. in the form of taxes)

**Gross domestic product (GDP) per capita:** the value per head of total output of the economy in a given period, divided by the population

**Gross National Product (GNP):** the value of goods and services produced in a given time period (e.g. one year) by labour and property supplied by residents of a country

## H

**Human Development Index (HDI):** measure of human well-being, consisting of three elements of human development: life expectancy, education and standard of living

## I

**Income elasticity:** responsiveness of demand to a change in income

**Income elasticity of demand:** measure of the responsiveness of demand to a change in income

**Indirect tax:** payment, such as taxes on the purchase of goods, made by an intermediary who passes the tax on to an end payer; the seller or producer pays these to the government but raises them initially from the consumer by setting a price that includes an amount to cover the tax

**Inelastic demand:** demand that changes by a smaller proportion than the change in price that instigated demand to change

**International Monetary Fund (IMF):** international body set up to provide finance for countries that need relatively short-term financial support (e.g. because they are not able to meet international debts in the short term)

**Invisible trade:** trade in services (e.g. banking, tourism, insurance, transport)

## J

**Joint supply:** two or more goods that are produced as part of the same production process (e.g. by-products created in the production of sugar from sugar cane, used as fuel for sugar mills)

**Joint venture:** an organisation jointly set up by two organisations; frequently set up when an international company wants to enter a new market

## L

**Law of comparative advantage:** helps to explain the gains from international trade. A country possesses a comparative advantage in the production of a good or service if it experiences lower opportunity cost in the production of that good or service

**Limited liability:** greatest amount that a company's owners might have to pay out to meet debts, the maximum being the sum that they invested in the business

## M

**Macro-economics/economy:** taking a broad view of the economy to consider, for example, the level of demand in the economy or the level of unemployment

**Marginal cost of production:** additional cost of producing one extra unit of a good

**Market:** any situation where buyers and sellers come into contact

**Market clearing price:** price at which the quantity supplied to the market will be bought in its entirety (with no unsatisfied demand)

**Market economy:** economy in which most economic decisions are made freely by private citizens, with only a limited amount of government interference

**Market equilibrium:** point at which demand and supply in the market are equal so that there is no tendency to change

**Marketing economies:** benefits resulting from carrying out marketing activities on a large scale (e.g. the cost of advertising a product globally can be spread over a large number of sales of the product)

**Merit good:** good that it is judged an individual should have on the basis of need (e.g. food provided to the poor through a public distribution system)

**Micro-economics/economy:** focusing on small-scale interactions between parts of the economy (e.g. how individual prices are determined)

**Mixed economy:** economy in which decisions are made through a combination of buyers and sellers deciding what to buy, produce and sell, coupled with some government interference, such as taxing or subsidising the production of some goods

**Monetary policy:** regulations created by the government and monetary authorities to control the supply of money in an economy and the level of interest rates

**Money supply:** total quantity of money

# Glossary

circulating in an economy at a particular moment in time; includes not only notes and coins but also other means of making payments

**Monopolistic competition:** situation in which there are many sellers producing similar but differentiated products

**Monopoly:** market controlled by a single supplier; businesses with monopoly powers are able to exercise some control over the supply to the market and the prices charged

## N

**National debt:** total of the financial obligations of a national government at a particular moment in time

**Normal profit:** profit that is the minimum required to keep a firm in a particular industry. It is equivalent to the opportunity cost of using the owner's capital in the next best alternative use

## O

**Oligopoly:** market structure in which there are a small number of firms operating in a market. They will either collude to set similar prices or compete vigorously with each other

**Opportunity cost:** next best alternative that is given up when a decision is made

**Optimum output:** output at which average cost is minimised

**Ordinary shares:** shares owned by a shareholder giving them an entitlement to a share in the profits of a company in the form of dividends

## P

**Perfect competition:** situation in which there are many buyers and sellers in a market, each of whom has knowledge of all of the prices being offered in the market; their products are identical, and new firms can readily enter or leave the market

**Perfectly inelastic supply:** supply that cannot change whatever the change in price

**Positive external effects or externalities:** benefits resulting from an economic decision being made that are in excess of the benefits gained by the individual or firm that makes an economic decision

**Price elasticity:** responsiveness of quantity demanded of a product to changes in price

**Price elasticity of demand:** responsiveness of quantity demanded to a change in the price of a specific item

**Price elasticity of supply:** responsiveness of quantity supplied to a change in the price of a specific item

**Price taker:** business that can only sell at the market price (i.e. a firm in a perfectly competitive market)

**Privatisation:** the transfer of a business from government to private ownership

**Producer goods:** goods bought by producers to enable them to produce goods (e.g. machinery)

**Production possibility curve:** line or curve showing possible combinations of two goods (or categories of goods) that can be produced using all existing resources in an economy

**Productivity:** relationship between the output of a good and the inputs contributed to make that good. It is measured by the quantity of output divided by the quantity of inputs

**Profit maximising:** point in the production or sales level at which there is the greatest difference between total revenue and total cost

**Public good:** product (e.g. street lighting), consumption of which by one person does not reduce the possibility of someone else consuming it and where no one can be excluded from consuming the good

## Q

**Quantitative easing:** situation whereby the monetary authorities (e.g. central bank) increase the quantity of money in the economy in order to encourage spending

## R

**Real asset:** asset that has intrinsic value in itself (e.g. gold or land)

**Recession:** two or more consecutive quarters (3-month periods) in which there is a fall in GDP

**Regulations:** rules and laws

**Revaluation:** where the government sets a new higher price for the domestic currency in terms of other exchange currencies

## S

**Shift in demand/supply curve:** effect of a change in factors other than the price of a good: a demand curve will shift to the right if a good becomes more popular or if consumers' incomes rise; a supply curve will shift to the right if technological improvements make it easier to produce that good

**Statement:** document setting out details of financial transactions, such as

withdrawals from a bank account

**Structural adjustment:** key changes that have to be made to the structure of the economy, often in order to comply with the requirements of foreign lenders (e.g. a country that borrows from the IMF may be 'encouraged' to privatise some of its industries)

**Structural unemployment:** unemployment resulting from a major restricting of industries in an economy (e.g. due to the shift from labour-intensive agriculture to capital-intensive manufacturing)

**Subsidies:** money granted by the state to keep down the price of goods and maintain the supply

**Supply:** quantity of a good that will be produced or sold at a particular price

## T

**Tariff:** sum of money that an importer or exporter has to pay to trade goods across borders

**Terms of trade:** price of exports divided by the price of imports

**Trade liberalisation:** opening up of trade between nations by lowering tariffs and reducing quota restrictions and other means

**Treasury bill:** paper document representing a short-term loan to the government. The central bank issues these and sells them on the money market

## U

**Unitary elasticity:** situation where the proportionate change in quantity demanded (or supplied) is equal to the proportionate change in price

## V

**Variable costs:** expenses that vary with the level of output (e.g. fuel costs, raw material costs)

**Visible trade:** exports and imports of physical goods

## W

**Weighting:** importance attached to items appearing in an index; the greater the weight, the more account is given to a particular factor that appears in an index

**World Trade Organisation (WTO):** international body supervising international trading; actively seeks to encourage removal of tariffs and quotas and to create regulations governing fair trading between nations

# Index